Biblical

Foundations

by

Harold McDougal

Laying Biblical Foundations:
How To Prepare Laborers For the Harvest
Copyright © 1997 — Harold McDougal
ALL RIGHTS RESERVED

All Scripture quotations are from
the Authorized King James Version of the Bible,
unless otherwise indicated.

PUBLISHED BY:

THE MCDOUGAL PUBLISHING COMPANY
P.O. Box 3595
HAGERSTOWN, MD 21742-3595

ISBN 1-884369-03-0

Printed in the United States of America
For worldwide distribution

Table of Contents

Introduction 5

Part I: The Formal Bible School Setting 13
 1. The Development of the Concept 15
 2. Is Bible Training Biblical? 21
 3. The Development of This Particular
    Program 25
 4. The Reasons For the Short-term
    Course 28
 5. The Methods Used 31
 6. The Teaching Method We Prefer 38
 7. The Proper Atmosphere 41
 8. The Right Facilities 43
 9. The Right Director 47
 10. The Right Teachers 49
 11. The Right Students 51
 12. The Right Subject Matter 57
 13. The Use of the Book *Principles of
    Christian Faith* 71

14.	The Use of Prepared Teaching Materials	74
15.	The Rules and Regulations For the Course	76
16.	Beginning	78
17.	The Screening of Students	83
18.	The Week of Prayer	88
19.	The Daily Schedule	92
20.	Preparation For the Classroom	96
21.	Testing	102
22.	Outside Activities	106
23.	Physical Work	109
24.	Sports?	112
25.	The Final Week	114
26.	The Field Training	116
27.	The Plan For Evangelization	120
28.	Materials For Evangelism	127
29.	The Graduation	130
30.	The Follow-up	132
31.	Paid or Free?	134
32.	A Word of Explanation on the Expulsion of Students	137

Part II: Adapting This System to Other Circumstances 143

33.	The Differences	145

The Appendix: Resource Materials For the Course 157

Introduction

Do you need more faithful workers in your church? It wouldn't be surprising if you did. With revival breaking out in many parts of our country and the world, the lack of qualified laborers is a fairly common problem.

If you are having that problem, where do you expect to get the workers? Will they just come to you in answer to prayer? Maybe.

Will they arrive already mature, conscientious, talented, self-sacrificing and hard working, like you need them to be? They might; but they probably won't.

As with everything else, Jesus is our example in this regard, and what He did constitutes an important biblical pattern to be followed.

Jesus didn't work alone. He chose faithful men whom He could prepare to work with Him and to carry on His work when He was gone. He didn't wait for those disciples to come to Him. He went out and handpicked them. Then He personally trained those He had selected, and this training consisted of the systematic laying down of proper biblical foundations.

Jesus taught His disciples by His example; He taught them by giving them some part in His ministry; and He taught them with His words. Much of the writings found in the Gospels are teachings that were not given to multitudes of people, but to a few chosen disciples.

Jesus spent a lot of time teaching His disciples, knowing that investing the time necessary to lay biblical foundations in the lives of these men would pay off in the long run; for they would be entrusted with the founding of the early Church.

Jesus took time to answer the questions His followers had because He knew that they would soon have to answer the questions of many other people. It was these rather ordinary men who would develop the New Testament teachings, teachings that would guide the Church through the centuries. Jesus took time to teach them well.

When these fledgling disciples failed in anything, Jesus helped them to see why they had failed and how to avoid the same failure in the future. And, when it was appropriate, He corrected them.

He was a spiritual father to the disciples, personally taking charge of their training, and the results were rewarding. Through this small group of men, the Christian message took hold, and the first-century church experienced a period of amazing growth.

That growth presented serious leadership problems, and the Apostles often found themselves in need of new leaders. Where did they get the leaders they needed?

They trained them, just as Jesus had done with them, taking the time to lay biblical foundations in each one of those who would be entrusted with leadership.

> *And daily in the temple, and in every house, they ceased not to teach ... .* Acts 5:42

The great Apostle Paul followed this same pattern of training for leadership. His success as a missionary was due to his custom of laying biblical foundations in the believers who were converted under his ministry:

> *Paul also and Barnabas continued in Antioch, teaching and preaching the word of the Lord, with many others also.* Acts 15:35

> *And he continued there a year and six months, teaching the word of God among them.*
> Acts 18:11

Paul's statement to the Ephesian elders shows his dedication to thoroughness in training those who were entrusted to his care:

> *I kept back nothing that was profitable unto you, but have shewed you, and have taught you publickly, and from house to house,* Acts 20:20

Paul continued this practice of carefully and systematically laying biblical foundations in new believers until the very end of his life. The final verse of the Acts of the Apostles powerfully reflects this fact:

> *Preaching the kingdom of God, and teaching those things which concern the Lord Jesus Christ, with all confidence, no man forbidding him.*
> Acts 28:31

It was this systematic biblical teaching that first developed the Christ-like spirit in men and women who loved the Lord and caused them to be known as *Christians:*

> *And when he [Barnabas] had found him [Paul], he brought him unto Antioch. And it came to pass, that a whole year they assembled themselves with the church, and taught much people. And the disciples were called Christians first in Antioch.*
> Acts 11:26

When the Bible speaks of the disciples *confirming* the believers, what they were actually doing was laying proper and complete foundations of truth in their converts so that they could withstand the storms of life and become fruitful in the Kingdom:

> *CONFIRMING the souls of the disciples, and exhorting them to continue in the faith, and that we must through much tribulation enter into the kingdom of God.* Acts 14:22

And Judas and Silas, being prophets also themselves, exhorted the brethren with many words, and CONFIRMED them. Acts 15:32

And he went through Syria and Cilicia, CONFIRMING the churches. Acts 15:41

The recognized responsibility of the first-century church was not only to win more souls to Christ, but to adequately train those who had already been won. And it was through this training that strong leadership emerged.

Now, in the closing years of the twentieth century, we find ourselves in a position similar to that of the early church. We are experiencing phenomenal growth and desperately need more and better leadership in our churches. Many, however, have been doing all the wrong things in this regard.

We keep waiting for the perfect people to come along, but God wants us to perfect the people we already have.

We keep waiting for talented people to come our way, but God wants us to lay hands on those we have and impart talents and abilities to them.

We keep criticizing our members because they don't help us enough, but God wants us to teach our members what they are to do and how they are to do it.

We have been relying on our modern concepts of leadership development, but God wants us to return to the way Jesus and the early Apostles developed leadership, by laying biblical foundations in the existing believers.

This ministry of laying biblical foundations did not end

with the first-century church. In every great revival, someone got a burden to train workers:

John Wesley had an army of circuit riders who were little Wesleys. They duplicated his ministry everywhere they went because He trained them. He was severely criticized by the Church of England (of which he was a part until his death) for using lay people. But the lay people Wesley chose got the job done, spreading Christ's teachings to every village of the New World.

William Booth, the founder of the Salvation Army, had disciplined and anointed officers in his troops, but they didn't just appear out of thin air. He trained them, and they took their world by storm. Can we expect it to be different for us today?

The very thought of you training your own workers may seem like an impossible task, but it is done one step at a time, one day at a time, one small investment after another — until the desired results are obtained.

The training concepts that are contained in this book were originally developed to help indigenous groups of national churches in foreign countries train their workers. They did this in established Bible schools or training centers. The system of training, however, is flexible and can be adapted to your own situation so that you can, for example, train workers right in your local church.

The teachings in this book deal principally with those who want to be full-time workers for the Lord and are, without a doubt, most effective when that type of commitment is made. You can, however, adapt them for teaching lay people, as well, as we shall see in Part II.

The course we designed requires six months of classroom study and six months of practical work in the field. You may shorten it or add to it, as needed.

Some of the materials we use are available in printed outline form in a book entitled *Principles of Christian Faith*. You may want to secure a copy, either as a study guide to be used in the classroom or as background material for the personal preparation of the teacher. Each individual subject also has resource material, and the Appendix contains a complete list of available materials.

The system we present here for training the workers you need is a proven one. It is based on the ministry of Jesus, the ministry of the Apostles, and the historical teachings of the Church down through the centuries. We believe it will bear fruit for you, as well.

The program is not set in stone, however. As members of the Body of Christ, we are all individuals and do things differently. Take from this teaching what is applicable to your own situation and trust God to give you whatever details may be lacking.

The important thing is to begin your training program. Don't delay any longer. The harvest is ripe. Accept the challenge to prepare more laborers for the great end-time harvest by **Laying Biblical Foundations**. I promise you that you will be revitalized in the process.

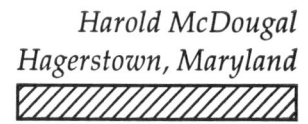

Harold McDougal
Hagerstown, Maryland

Part I:

LAYING BIBLICAL FOUNDATIONS

The Formal Bible School Setting

- 1 -

LAYING BIBLICAL FOUNDATIONS
The Development of the Concept

Since most of my experience has been in the formal Bible school setting, let me begin there. Later, in Part II, we will suggest ways to adapt this system of training to other circumstances.

In the early years of our missionary ministry, while we were living and working in the Philippines, we felt there was no time for Bible training for our co-workers. We could sense the rapid passing of time and see the visible harvest waiting to be reaped. This compelled us to utilize every available person in the ministry — young people, lay people and even new converts.

Looking back now, I don't think we were wrong in believing that everyone could be used in the harvest. I still believe that. But we were wrong in believing that untrained people would always be faithful, would always maintain a good testimony and would be able to teach others — considering their own limited background.

Finding areas that had never been evangelized, we formed new congregations through evangelistic crusades, then put whoever we could find in charge of them. You can imagine what happened to some of those new congregations. They didn't grow. How could they? Hungry souls were not being properly fed. Individual problems were not being properly dealt with. Local leadership was not being developed. So it was only a matter of time before attendance, strong right after the crusade ended, began to diminish.

"Church attendance" is not an inanimate phrase. It doesn't refer only to numbers. It represents people, precious souls. During the time of our experimentation, some believers disappeared from view, never to reappear again, and we felt that we were to blame and considered it to be an awesome responsibility!

It was naïve of us to believe that a person of limited experience and training could carry such a great responsibility — that of parenting a large group of newborn babes, a job that demands maturity and wisdom. Some of our "workers" were unable to face persecution. Some had no idea what to do in response to difficulty. Some of them never learned to walk by faith and couldn't believe God for their personal needs. Thrust into an impossible situation, some of them eventually got discouraged and quit and some did foolish or childish things that hurt their testimonies.

This turn of events forced us to rethink our total posi-

The Development of the Concept

tion and to consider the need for systematic Bible training. We had to do something. Reluctantly, we prepared some crude facilities on a donated property, in the mountains away from the city, secured some experienced teachers from another spirit-filled group, and began a training program.

It wasn't easy. Everyone had their preconceived ideas about what should be taught and why. There was little consensus on anything: the daily schedule, the rules, the length of the course, the type of services to be held or who was to teach what. The worse thing, to me, was that the whole process seemed to be so slow and drawn out. We struggled on in this way for two years, improving our facilities in the process, but were still disturbed by the lack of immediate results.

During those years, we were crying out to God for an answer to this dilemma. We were operating the type of Bible school we had vowed never to operate, while many towns and villages needed pastors and many unevangelized areas waited for the Gospel message. Could we afford to do what others before us had done: allow anointed young people who were called to the ministry to sit in a classroom and die? I continued to ask the Lord to show us how we could effectively prepare laborers for the harvest — quickly. God heard that cry and answered in a very unusual way.

A great storm swept our area and tore down the buildings we had constructed for the Bible school. Fortunately, no one was killed. Other than one broken wrist and a few missing teeth, the students and teachers were miraculously spared. The buildings, however, were severely damaged. One of them was a total loss, while the largest, a U-shaped two-story building, lost the second floor and roof.

There wasn't time to think right then about what to do next. We had a large student body with teachers and teachers' families — all left homeless by the storm. Their meager possessions were scattered over a radius of many miles. We took the students, their teachers and their families into the city to sleep, eat, and pray in one of the church buildings. There was no other alternative for the moment. I definitely did not feel that we should give up the whole training project. We desperately needed faithful workers. We simply had to go on — somehow.

A few days after the storm I had to take a long bus ride north to dedicate a new church. I felt that the long ride would give me a chance to sort out my thoughts. It did. An unusual thing happened that day.

A rainbow appeared in the sky on my side of the bus and followed us all day long, as we moved north across the island. I never lost sight of it throughout the day. I don't know about the scientific probability of that happening. I only know that it happened to me.

As I watched that beautiful rainbow, the Lord spoke to me. He told me not to be sad because the existing Bible school buildings had been destroyed. He said that He had something better in mind for us and that we would soon see the benefits of what He had done.

This was confirmed later, in prophecy, when the Lord said that the destruction of the Bible school buildings had a divine purpose and that if we tried to rebuild them before the right time, He would tear them down again.

The Development of the Concept

When I got back to the capital from that trip north, I was very excited. I knew that God was giving us a chance to break out of the old mold into something new and exciting.

We rented two apartments near the church, one for the men and one for the women, and continued our Bible training program. Because of the storm and its aftermath and because of an upcoming crusade, we made some serious changes in our program. We decided to drop our regular classes for the moment and enter into an intensive period of seeking God and allowing Him to speak to us. The teachers and some visiting missionaries joined us. We spent a lot of time just learning how to worship the Lord.

We decided to continue the suspension of our normal schedule and get the students totally involved in a series of evangelistic crusades. They worked very hard physically with the preparation for those crusades, while continuing a full schedule of prayer and study. There were both positive and negative results.

The cramped quarters at first brought out the worst in everyone. There were some complaints, some unkind words, and some near fist fights. A few of the students dropped out of the group and went home. By the time we began traveling to the various crusades, therefore, the group was a little smaller. But those who remained began to blossom.

In each city that we visited, we continued daily prayer and teaching sessions. In the crusade meetings, the students testified, sang, and ministered to the spiritually hungry people.

Within a few months of this intensive training which included both systematic teaching and the practical application of that teaching, there was a remarkable change in those who stuck it out. Of that group, a good number became missionaries and went out to minister to other countries. Others became teachers and preachers and developed their own ministries, founded churches and established their own training programs. Most of them are still serving the Lord very faithfully more than twenty-five years later.

It was in this way that the Lord taught us some of the secrets of preparing laborers for His harvest field, *Laying Biblical Foundations*. In the following years, we put this system to work on several continents, each time with equally fruitful results.

- 2 -

LAYING BIBLICAL FOUNDATIONS
Is Bible Training Biblical?

There is so much disagreement in the church today over whether or not we actually need Bible training. At one extreme, liberals scorn Bible schools. To them, Bible schools represent "the lazy man's way of avoiding seminary training." What we see coming out of our seminaries, however, does not always inspire us. Genuine faith in God and His Word are mocked in many of our major seminaries, and those who graduate from these programs are not always fruitful for the Kingdom.

At the other extreme, there are ultraconservatives who shun Bible school as "man's teachings." They believe in just letting the Spirit teach us everything. Some actually put a premium on ignorance, believing it to be unspiritual to learn. If this is true, why did God place teachers in the Church?

A wise older missionary from New Zealand who helped me in the early years of my missionary ministry taught me that the ministry must be a balance of the Spirit and the Word. Those who are zealous in the Spirit, but who don't know the Word, often fall into error, while those who can recite the Word backward and forward, but don't have the Spirit, minister dryness (see 2 Corinthians 3:6). The ideal is to have a person who is both sensitive to the Spirit and knowledgeable in the Word!

So, is Bible training or Bible school biblical? We must admit that we cannot find the term "Bible school" in the Scriptures. We find only what is commonly called *the school of the prophets* which existed in Old Testament times (2 Kings 2:5, 4:38 & 6:1). Nothing else resembling our modern Bible schools appears, either in the Old or New Covenants.

How were the ministers of the New Testament prepared for their work? Jesus trained the first twelve Himself and commanded them to teach their converts everything that He had taught them (see Matthew 28:20). They, in obedience, taught the Church (see Acts 2:40).

Still, no point was made, in early church history, of separating out a few individuals for special training, as we do today. The entire membership of the Church was trained in the Word and the ministry of the Spirit. Then, from among the members of the local church, elders (the more spiritually mature ones) were chosen to pastor the flock. Jerusalem did not send out pastors for each local church. Pastors and other church leaders were appar-

Is Bible Training Biblical?

ently raised up in each locale. So, a case could be made that Bible schools are not really biblical.

In fact, what we know today as "Bible school," for the most part, is not very biblical. Many Bible schools have lost the New Testament vision. Instead of providing a place where men and women can seek God and prepare for the ministry, they have established institutions of higher learning. And, since education and enlightenment are not the same, this is unacceptable.

If a Bible school, Bible college, or Bible institute becomes a place to further one's education, it ceases to fulfill the goals set for us by the Lord. Because of this, we often chose to avoid the use of these terms, and just to call our programs *training centers*.

There *is* a need for teaching in the church today, and teaching *all things* that the Lord commanded is part of the Great Commission. It would be ideal if the entire membership of the church learned the Word of God and became effective ministers for God, as the members of the first-century church apparently did. But this is not the case today.

In the closing years of the twentieth century, people are busy with their personal lives and feel they cannot give the time necessary to learn the Word of God effectively. It has become our custom, therefore, to take those who want to give themselves completely to God's service and group them into schools or training programs. This is certainly biblical.

Any Bible training program, whatever it is called, may degenerate into a useless program, or it may maintain its life-changing character. So, there are good and bad Bible schools, just as there are good and bad churches and good and bad preachers. The concept of the Church is biblical; the concept of the preacher is biblical; and the concept of the Bible school or Bible training center, a place dedicated to preparing leaders among God's people to do the work of the Church, is also biblical.

Liberals would have us spend too many years in higher education. This is clearly not pleasing to the Lord. Ultra-conservatives, on the other hand, would have us believe that everything comes automatically as a gift from God. This is clearly not the case. Jesus taught the disciples; and they, in turn, taught the Church. Teachers were part of God's gift to the Church and must be given their proper place in His plan.

It is time to accept our responsibility and begin *Laying Biblical Foundations*. Nothing could be more biblical and nothing could be more pleasing to God.

- 3 -

LAYING BIBLICAL FOUNDATIONS
The Development of This Particular Program

Each of us has learned from others. Before going to the mission field, I had the privilege of sitting at the feet of my pastor, Vernon W. Miles, Sr., of reading the good books of W. V. Grant, Sr., and of attending the meetings of Katherine Kuhlman and Oral Roberts. Later, I was blessed by knowing, receiving the ministries, and reading the books of such well known ministers as T. L. Osborn, Morris Cerullo, Gordon Lindsay, A. A. Allen, Richard Wurmbrand, Luis Palau, Paul Finkenbinder (Hermano Pablo), the Heflin family and others.

The teachings that we began to impart to others, I am sure, owed much to each of these dedicated servants of God. These men and women all had something in common. Not many of them were eloquent orators. They had a very simple message, but it was powerful because they lived it. They inspired us to do the same.

I was aided by the fact that the people I was ministering to did not have English as their mother tongue. I quickly learned to avoid all "play on words." Word studies, which I had loved as a youth, sometimes reading from five or six different translations to get the various shades of meaning, now gave way to a much simpler and practical approach to the Gospel. All the embellishment was cut away so that we could quickly get to the root of the matter. And this search for simplicity proved to be an important key to the development of the program.

At first, nothing was written. I wanted to give fresh teachings to my students; so I prepared daily, making only a few notes (as reminders to myself). This was okay at the beginning, but as my responsibilities in the work grew and I had less time to prepare, or when I had to put another teacher over a particular course and had nothing to give them as a guide, this lack of written material became a problem.

While living in Ecuador, I began to put my teachings into simple outline form that I could later pass along to others. I still prefer for a gifted teacher to prepare his or her own teaching materials, but not everyone has the gift of systematically covering the necessary material without spending too much time on nonessentials; and those teachers need our help.

The outlines that I prepared were later translated into English and edited.

In the winter of 1984-85, I used those outlines to help a large local church establish a training center in Sierra

The Development of This Particular Course

Leone, West Africa, and the following year the materials first appeared in printed form. It was entitled *Principles of Christian Faith, Volume I.*

As I was preparing to work with the teachers in Freetown, I realized there were many details that the Lord had graciously taught us through the years that someone just beginning a training program would have no way of knowing. During my free hours the week of the crusade, just before the opening of the training center, I began to put these thoughts down on paper, and thus developed *The Guide For Teachers*. That *Guide* forms the basis for this present volume, although periodically I have added some new insight to these materials or clarified them in some way.

The program that we present here is flexible. It may be adapted to local situations, situations that vary drastically, depending on where you are in the world. But the system works just as well in Asia, Latin America, Africa, or our Western nations. And it will work for YOU. Prepare yourself to start **Laying Biblical Foundations.**

- 4 -

LAYING BIBLICAL FOUNDATIONS
The Reasons For the Short-term Course

The course of study that we propose is not a short course, but an *intensive* short-term course. The first twenty-six weeks alone include 195 hours of prayer, 26 days of fasting, 780 hours of teaching, memorization of 120 verses, and participation in some 78 services. If the same material were studied for an hour and a half, 1 night a week, 40 weeks of the year, it would take more than 12 years to finish the course.

Training takes a lot of time, just as we cannot raise our children in a few weeks or a few months. It takes years of full-time attention to the many details of our children's development to see the desired results, and we cannot do less for the servants of God and of His Church.

The Reasons For the Short-term Course

Training, however, does not have to take many years. It can be done in a short period through intensive techniques. This could be likened to the important formative years of childhood, when we learn the essentials that will guide us through the rest of our lives. It is also similar to boot camp for soldiers or to many on-the-job training programs that have proven so popular and useful to industry.

There are many reasons we prefer the short-term course of Bible training:

1. A lengthy training program is, we believe, incompatible with our knowledge of the coming of Christ. If we really believe He is coming back, how can we spend years preparing to warn people? We must warn them NOW.

2. The Christian worker has been ordained by God to *bring forth fruit* (John 15:16). If he (or she) sits for a long period of time without bearing fruit, he grows cold and indifferent, until even his own spiritual experience is affected. Large numbers of seminary graduates change their minds about ministry and go into business, politics or the professions — because they have lost the burden for the Lord's work during an extended training period.

3. Intellectualism is contrary to spirituality. Although knowledge need not interfere with our spiritual experience, the general rule is that those

who study theology for long periods of time lose the simplicity of their faith in God.

4. Knowledge often leads to pride, and *pride goeth before destruction* (Proverbs 16:18).

5. Long-term Bible training is incompatible with the need. It is harvest time. When the natural harvest is ready, we don't want to lose any time. In many countries even children and grandparents are called upon to help reap the precious grain. It is not a time to send anyone off to agricultural school. The grain is in danger of falling to the ground and being eternally lost.

6. On-the-job training has proven to be the most economical and practical method of preparation for many professions. We are stewards of God's time, God's talents, and God's money. The short-term training program produces more workers, faster and more economically, than any other type of training.

These are among the reasons we feel the intensive short-term program of training best serves the interests of those involved in revival all over the world. In this way, *Laying Biblical Foundations* may be done quickly, economically and effectively.

LAYING BIBLICAL FOUNDATIONS
The Methods Used

Bible training is not the same as factory training, agricultural training, or professional training. It is not simply reciting facts and memorizing lists. It is imparting the grace and power of God to others. The methods, therefore, cannot be carnal.

The methods used in this course are spiritual — fasting and prayer, personal and group discipline, preaching and teaching, reproof and rebuke etc. Those applying the methods must be spiritual in order to effectively give out, and those accepting the application must be spiritual in order to effectively receive.

The most important goal of the course is not the memorization of Bible verses, nor the ability to intellectually explain doctrines, but the ability to develop a deep, personal relationship with the Lord, to become sensitive to the Spirit's leading, to hear (literally) the voice of God, and to develop the discipline to obey what He is saying.

Fasting

In order to encourage students to develop a habit of fasting and prayer, we should institute fast days during the course of the program. There should be at least one full day of fasting each week.

Although how and when the fast is observed is somewhat flexible, I personally prefer that the students and teachers eat no solid foods from the time they arise one day until breakfast of the following day. They may take water or, if their concept of fasting permits, an occasional tea, coffee, or juice.

It would be perfectly proper for the director or pastor (if he is not the same person) to call for two or three days of complete fasting (taking neither food nor drink) at any time during the course of the training. Some churches only fast in this way, and that's fine. Whatever your personal concept of fasting is, do it!

Requiring the students to fast one complete day a week, at least, is important because fasting is an important biblical principle and because those who are unwilling to fast and seek God set a limit on the depth of spirituality they can reach.

Fasting has many benefits for the students. It will enable them to better enter into prayer, to clear their minds of hindrances to study, and to discipline themselves. Those students who are unwilling to fast, therefore, should be dismissed from the course. There may be some exceptions, such as for students who have diabetes, but these can be dealt with on a case-by-case basis.

The teachers, administrators and staff must set a proper example in fasting.

Prayer

The knowledge of the Word which the students acquire during the program must be balanced by a deep, personal relationship with the Lord. Regular prayer times open the student's spirit and understanding for the day's learning. Those who do not learn to pray sincerely and earnestly will not be able to absorb the amount of teaching offered in the intensive, short-term program. The morning should begin with a full hour of prayer and the afternoon with another, shorter period of prayer.

The students should arrive early for services to pray and should pray around the altars at the close of each service. Any student who is not "pressing into" prayer should be counseled and prayed for. If the problem hindering a student cannot be resolved, he may eventually have to be dismissed. Nothing may be allowed to hinder the progress of other students, and each student must develop the godly habit of prayer.

Personal Discipline

During the twenty-six weeks of classroom activity, each student should be required to develop a personal discipline. This will be accomplished through strict obedience to the rules and regulations for the course — which include a full day of fasting each week, assigned chores and work days, respect for leaders and one another, attendance at all prayer times, classes, services, meal times and extra activities, being on time always, and being properly dressed at all times, among other things.

When it is noticed that discipline has been breached, the teacher or director should immediately call the attention of the student to the problem. If the problem persists, expulsion must be considered as the best thing for the good of the whole group.

The flesh resists discipline, and if you make it too easy for your students to avoid this all-important part of the training, you will do them irreparable harm spiritually. Their discipline as a group must lead to a disciplined life for them as individuals once they have graduated from the program.

The Memorization of Scriptures

One assigned verse should be memorized by the students each day. The previous days' verses can be reviewed to assure that they "stick." If this is done, by the end of the 26 weeks, some 120 verses will have been memorized; and the student will have formed a new, positive thought life. Some students will find this difficult, but all should be required to do it, as it is for their benefit.

An additional 120 verses may be assigned to be memorized during the field training period, if desired.

Reading and Reporting

Since an important part of the ministry is the ability to absorb information from other sources and pass it on to others in a meaningful form, the students will be required, as part of their Language Improvement class, to read at least one good book each month, as well as newspapers and current events magazines, and to present oral and/or written reports on what they have read. (Since newspapers are unreliable in some countries, due caution should be expressed.)

Testing

Testing is a normal part of life. Students, therefore, should be tested. They should be tested sometimes without warning. They should always be tested at the end of each subject presented and at the end of their classroom training period.

The teachers should discourage cramming for these exams. Students should not be permitted, for example, to stay up all night before an exam. They must discipline themselves to master the material on a daily basis and learn that testing is a normal part of the daily life, to be faced with courage and strength.

Teaching/Preaching

In some circles, the difference between teaching and preaching is hotly debated. The difference, certainly, should not be in the enthusiasm and anointing with which the material is presented. The teacher should never sit calmly behind a desk while teaching the eternal truths of God's Word. Although the teaching should be done in a systematic and orderly fashion, without straying from the subject (unless the teacher is specifically led to do so), the lesson must be presented with power and authority.

Lengthy class discussion is necessarily limited in a short-term course. Occasional questions may be entertained; but, for the most part, students should be encouraged to write down their questions as they occur to them, so as not to forget them, and to have those questions ready for a designated question-and-answer period.

During such question-and-answer periods, controversial and speculative subjects should be avoided (unless the teacher has some clear insight that can quickly bring the discussion to a conclusion). There is nothing wrong with a teacher occasionally saying, "I don't know," and it is wrong to waste time on speculative matters to which there may be no "correct answer."

When addressing controversial issues, each teacher should be discreet and not entertain discussions of what another teacher has said in another class. Teachers will disagree on minor issues. Their points of disagreement should never, however, become public debate. If you were not present when the teachings in question were given and, therefore, don't know exactly what was said, it is better to decline comment and avoid discussions over differences of opinion.

If teachers consistently put forth opposing views on major doctrinal points, it may confuse the students and cause them to lose interest in their classes, as well as respect for their teachers. At the slightest hint of major differences among teachers, the director should call the teachers together and clarify to them the official position of the school on the matter. If a teacher is unwilling to abide by the official position, he should withdraw or be

The Methods Used

dismissed, since we are dealing with eternal values and cannot afford to be lenient in this regard.

Parenting

The most important aspect of the training is that the teachers must become spiritual fathers and mothers to the students. We must be constantly concerned about their progress and their problems. We must share their joys and their sorrows. We take them under our wings and do for them exactly what we have done for our own physical children—raise them (spiritually).

A willingness to parent others is, of course, the ideal, and not everyone is willing to make the necessary sacrifices to cause this technique to work successfully. But this is what the Lord is asking of us:

> *For though ye have ten thousand instructors in Christ, yet have ye not many fathers.*
>
> 1 Corinthians 4:15

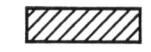

Get ready for *Laying Biblical Foundations.*

- 6 -

LAYING BIBLICAL FOUNDATIONS
The Teaching Method We Prefer

The method of Bible study that we prefer to use in laying biblical foundations is based on the belief that the Bible is its own best commentary. In other words, the Bible explains itself. If you have difficulty understanding a certain Bible passage, then reading several similar biblical passages will usually clarify your thinking on the subject.

Most false doctrines are based on a single passage of Scripture (usually taken out of context). If you read a variety of passages related to the same topic, the truth God wants to reveal becomes more clear; and, as a result, the false doctrine is revealed as error.

Those who can read the Bible in several languages have

The Teaching Method We Prefer

a great advantage here. Many people agree that if you read a passage of the Bible in several languages, its meaning becomes clearer. For those who don't have the luxury of knowing more than one language and who need a good substitute, reading several related passages (for instance: one from the books of Moses, one from the Psalms, one from the Prophets, one from the words of Jesus, and one from Paul) may be the best available substitute.

When you read God's Word in public, do it with excitement and expectancy. If you are leading a group, you may want to have members of the group stand and read the verses you want to emphasize. Have them do it with enthusiasm and anointing. The Word of God is never boring.

When you are laying biblical foundations — whether in an individual or a group — do it completely. Don't skip a particular subject simply because it doesn't interest you or because you think it may not interest the group. If you feel personally confident that the members of the group you are teaching is well founded in a particular doctrinal area, you may not need to spend as much time on that teaching as you otherwise would. But don't be guilty of frustrating the system by skipping around to the "goodies," the things you think people want to hear or things that seem more interesting. Lay a complete foundation. There will be time later for adornment.

When using the book *Principles of Christian Faith* to prepare yourself for teaching a particular subject, you will want to read all or most of the passages in a particular lesson. You may then decide which passages you want to use in the formal setting. I don't encourage anyone to stand in front of a group of people and read from one of my outlines a line at a time. Study the material and make it your own; then teach it in your own way — in the Spirit, thus *Laying Biblical Foundations*.

LAYING BIBLICAL FOUNDATIONS
The Proper Atmosphere

The local church was the Bible school of the New Testament; and today, nearly two thousand years later, the local church is still the best atmosphere for the training of men and women in Bible truths. If the Bible school is taken out of the local church and isolated in some remote area, it will not produce the same results. Having a training center which is isolated, even if you have regular prayer, chapel services, and outstation activities for the students, is no substitute for the atmosphere of the local church.

While it is true that the students need to pray together and interact together, they also need the fellowship, the moral and financial support, and the opportunity to minister that the local church provides.

It is not only the students who benefit from this relationship. The church members are blessed by the presence, the testimony, and the ministry of the students. These zealous warriors lend a new fire and enthusiasm to the congregation, and the members are challenged by their dedication.

The members of the church should be encouraged to attend the morning prayer and meditation and, at times, even selected classes. Let the members take pride in this ministry. If you can accomplish this, your members will give more and pray more, as a result.

Of course, to provide the proper atmosphere for such a training program, the local church must have a good testimony; it must be a praying church with a wide variety of activities; it must have freedom for the gifts of the Spirit to develop; and it must have instructive and fruit-bearing services. In such an atmosphere, spiritual children will grow quickly, and you can concentrate on *Laying Biblical Foundations.*

- 8 -

LAYING BIBLICAL FOUNDATIONS
The Right Facilities

Jesus had a traveling Bible school, and His students had no assurance of even a place to lay their heads. They sat on the grass of the hillside or on a rock by the lake as He taught. The physical facility, we could then conclude, is not really very important.

Prayer and teaching, however, must be done in a place of few distractions. Jesus went into a desert place or up on a mountain *apart* (Matthew 14:13, 23 & 17:1). Children playing or a nearby construction project, for example, can be tools of the devil to snatch the precious seed away from students who are trying in vain to concentrate on what they are learning. Remember that we are dealing with eternal values and must not let small things rob the students.

Several other things are helpful when considering the right facilities:

The Classroom and Its Furnishings

The teaching place should be well ventilated, well lighted and neither too hot nor too cold. No matter where it is, if there is activity outside the door, that can prove to be distractive, and the door should be shut.

The teaching might simply be done in the sanctuary of the church. Many church sanctuaries are only used at service times and being able to use them for a training program for those who aspire to ministry helps to justify the investment you have made in such sanctuaries. I personally prefer to have the morning prayer, the meditation, and the first class of the day in such a setting so that the other members of the congregation may participate.

I choose not to interrupt the spirit of this early-morning time unless forced to move for some other activity that needs the space. At the morning break, the class may move to a smaller room — if it is available.

The chairs or benches on which the students sit day after day should have a back, since the students will be required to study for hours at a time. If they have a small desktop it is better, but it is not essential.

In our electronic age, many schools are using various teaching aids. If these are available, take advantage of them. However, they are not required. Don't just try to copy what someone else is doing in this regard. Do what seems right for you.

The Right Facilities

Sleeping, Eating, and Bathing Facilities

The sleeping, eating and bathing facilities for the students do not need to be luxurious. Those students who have sacrificed most in the past seem to actually turn out to be better servants of God in the long run.

The Sleeping Facilities:
>Students need to learn to live with others in close surroundings, so four to eight students to a room is good. One large dormitory for all the men and another for the ladies is also acceptable.
>
>All the facilities should be clean and well-ordered to begin with, and the students should be expected to maintain them in this condition.

The Eating Facilities:
>The cooking and eating areas may be extremely simple. They may be open (where the weather permits), roofed (in areas of hot sun), or enclosed simply in colder areas. Benches or chairs may be moved from place to place, as needed.

The Bathing and Clothes Washing Facilities:
>Thought should be given to the need for the students to all bathe and change clothes within a short period before services. Provision should be made for adequate clean water and space for several students to bathe and/or wash clothes at one time.

Other Facilities

If there is an open space available where the students may relax sometimes with a basketball, football or volleyball or just walk or run, it may be helpful. If there is an area where a ping pong table can be set up for their use or an area where students can play chess, checkers, scrabble or other wholesome and challenging games, it can go a long way toward helping them to relax during their free time. If any or all of these facilities are unavailable, don't worry about it. Make the best use of what you have, as you dedicate yourself to the task of *Laying Biblical Foundations.*

- 9 -

LAYING BIBLICAL FOUNDATIONS
The Right Director

To effectively run a ministerial training program, you need a director, someone in charge. This director should be a man when possible, but if a woman is more qualified, use her.

Often the pastor of the church will make the best director. He understands the vision of the church and what it hopes to accomplish through such a training program. If the pastor feels that his time is too limited to serve in this capacity, he may suggest someone else.

The director should be a unique person, must understand the purposes and the techniques of the training program and must be able to put into effect whatever is necessary to achieve your goals. He must be a person of experience and vision, so that he will be respected by teachers and students alike.

The director must have the wisdom to choose teachers to help him, to assign each teacher a subject, to oversee their work, and to periodically make any necessary adjustments in the staff without offending, if possible, the other teachers and students.

Since teachers have differing views, it falls to the director to express the official position of the church and see that the official position is taught.

To the director falls the responsibility of disciplining unruly students. He must have both strictness and compassion to discipline the erring. If a student cannot be helped, it is the director's responsibility to dismiss that student before others are adversely affected.

The director must set dates and make schedules after conferring with other teachers and the pastor (if the pastor is not the director). The input of others is useful; but, since others often do not have an opinion to share, the director must be ready to make major decisions without much outside help.

The director will review any outside material that is to be presented to the students, especially when it is doctrinal in nature. He will approve any change in schedule, subject matter, or teachers.

The director must be involved in the day-to-day activities of the center. It does not work well to have a director who is in charge but detached from the reality of the situation. Believe God to give you such a person, or believe God to make you such a person so that you can get serious about *Laying Biblical Foundations.*

- 10 -

LAYING BIBLICAL FOUNDATIONS
The Right Teachers

The teachers used in an intensive short-term Bible training program are unlike teachers in the secular sense.

First, these men and women must be examples for the students to emulate. If the teachers don't fast, don't pray, are not self-disciplined, or if they arrive late, or do not regard regulations, the students will adopt these bad traits. No more can be expected of the students than of the teachers. The teachers, therefore, must be born-again, spirit-filled, called and "on fire" for God.

Teachers who are chosen to train future ministers must have a world vision. A teacher with a limited vision will only hinder the students' progress.

The teacher must be experienced. If he has never experienced the things he is teaching, the teaching will seem hollow and will have little impact on the students. Therefore, a teacher must speak, for the most part, from experience. He must be a fruit bearer. If not, the students will not be challenged by him to develop their own ministries.

The teacher should be gifted. God put teachers in the Church. Generally speaking, college professors often do not make good trainers. They tend to rely on their intellectual ability instead of seeking God and giving a spiritual presentation.

There are those in the Church who have received a special gift for teaching. (Not necessarily the same as a natural or developed ability to teach school.) If we can identify these gifted men and women and use them, they will do a good job for us.

Part-time teachers — for example, businessmen or professionals — often do not make good teachers for a course such as this. The students wonder: If this person believes what he teaches, why doesn't he leave all, as the original disciples did, and follow the Lord? Since the students are giving themselves full-time to the Lord's work, people who have done the same must be put before them as role models.

Believe God to give you anointed teachers, and believe God to make you an anointed teacher so that you can get on with the task of *Laying Biblical Foundations.*

- 11 -

LAYING BIBLICAL FOUNDATIONS
The Right Students

It is good to train each member of the church. In fact, it is our duty to do so. As the majority of the members, however, are lay people, we must teach them on a schedule convenient to them. Although this course may be used in that way, it was designed as an intensive training for those who have a special calling and make themselves one hundred percent available to God. It is clear in the Scriptures that the twelve *forsook their nets, and followed Him* (Mark 1:18).

Full-time students and part-time students should not be mixed. This course is designed for a full-time, intensive, six-month study for those who wish to give themselves to full-time service to the Lord. A very different approach must be used for lay people (See Part II).

Not every student who applies for training can be accepted. There are many reasons for this. The two most important are:

1. One bad student, one who is carnal or insincere, can adversely affect the entire group.

2. As good stewards, we must be mindful to use wisely God's money and the investment of the time and talent of His servants, as well.

The students for this course, therefore, should be carefully selected on the basis of the following criteria:

Their Experience

In a personal interview, the students should be asked to relate how they received Christ. If they cannot do that, they probably have not experienced the new birth.

Have they received the Holy Ghost baptism? If not, why not? Do they believe in the Holy Ghost baptism? Are they actively seeking this experience?

The student's response to these questions will help you to determine their spiritual experiences.

Their Calling

If a student merely wants to further his education, he should not be accepted into this course. A good way to ascertain the student's intent is to ask: "What do you plan to do after you finish this course?" If the answer is:

The Right Students

"continue my education," "return to my profession," or something similar, it becomes obvious that this person does not yet feel the calling to full-time service that is so important right now to world evangelism.

Ask the students to explain their calling. If it is real, they will be able to express their feelings — even if they don't use all the right words. Don't expect a young person to know specifically what role he or she will play in the Body of Christ. Many mature believers still do not know after being in the Church for years.

It shouldn't take you long to establish in your own spirit the validity of the calling of those who apply.

Their Willingness

Although the students may be young, immature, and lacking in knowledge, they can learn if they are willing to work hard and to discipline themselves. They should be told that the course is demanding and asked if they are willing to submit themselves completely to such a strict discipline. Are they serious enough to complete such an intensive course? If not, this program is not for them.

Be moved as much by what you feel as by what you hear from each prospective student in this regard. The Spirit of God is faithful to show us the sincerity of men's hearts.

Their Attitude

Are the students respectful and cooperative? These are essential ingredients for those who will be molded into effective servants of God. Students who are lacking respect for others, especially those in authority, and who are lacking a cooperative spirit will only burden the program; and you are better off without them.

Student Selection

The responsibility of selecting the right students, of course, falls on those in charge, and it is an awesome task. Turn away the wrong students, and you are denying them an opportunity to develop their talents and abilities for God. Accept the wrong students, and you are hindering the rest of the group in their progress and risking the very testimony of the church and its training center.

Choices such as these must be made in the Spirit, with much fasting and prayer, and by two or three Spirit-led people. The director should have the final word, taking the responsibility of making the selections.

Once the choices are made, leave the matter with God. It is easy to worry about having done right or wrong and the effect such a decision might have on the future of a particular young person. It is also not uncommon for casual observers to disagree with the decisions made. Make your choices in prayer, and leave the results to the Lord.

Accepting Women

In some countries women are not yet accepted as ministers and, therefore, are not accepted as Bible students.

The Right Students

The Bible teaches, however, that *there is neither male nor female* in Christ (Galatians 3:28). The early church had deaconesses, prophetesses and women in other ministerial positions. Paul gave honor to Phebe and other important women of the church (Romans 16:1-2).

We should encourage both males and females to prepare for the ministry — if necessary being pioneers in our respective nations for the acceptance of women in ministry.

While the Scriptures teach that it is better for a man to have a position of authority (when good men are available), this in no way closes women out of ministry. Many women, when given an opportunity, do better than men. Give your women the opportunity they deserve.

Accepting only men does not keep those men from temptation. The world is not segregated, and male students will soon meet women everywhere they go, so they must learn now to deal with women justly and morally.

Strict rules of discipline and careful supervision will protect the church and its training center from scandals arising over boy/girl relationships.

The Continuing Process

Because it is sometimes difficult to make a sound decision about a person after observing them over a short period, the process of evaluating a student will continue, even for those who are accepted into the program. During the first week, especially, there should be a close observation of the students. Are they praying and seeking God? Are they humble? Are they getting along well together? Any serious problems that surface should be dealt with immediately; and any student who shows a lack of response in these areas should be sent home. These are essential ingredients to success in the ministry, and if they are totally lacking in an individual, there is little hope of progress for that person.

In Chapter 15, we will discuss how to get the students you need so that you can get busy *Laying Biblical Foundations.*

- 12 -

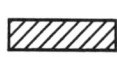

LAYING BIBLICAL FOUNDATIONS
The Right Subject Matter

What to teach in the limited time available in a short-term course is not an easy decision. This is compounded by the fact that each teacher takes a little different approach to teaching. I personally feel that many Christians err in trying to leap over the basics of the faith into the exciting subjects of the gifts of the Spirit and future events. While it is possible to take great leaps in the Spirit, the Bible clearly shows us that the house which lacks a proper foundation is doomed to fall. We must never take anything for granted in the preparation of God's servants, and must, therefore, lay a complete foundation.

Of the dozens of subjects generally taught in Bible

schools, the following seem, to me, to be foundation material:

The Principles

The doctrinal truths we present in the book, under the heading, **The Principles,** cover, in the simplest way possible, all the major doctrines of the Bible. For the most part, I have attempted in this study to avoid controversial subjects and present only the basic Christian truths — to which the majority of the Church fathers have adhered down through the centuries. This course covers everything from *God, Man, Sin* and *Salvation*, to *Predestination, Prosperity,* and *the Life of Faith.*

Each subject is concise. In many schools, an entire course would be taught, for example, on Christology. We spend anywhere from one class period to four or five class periods at the most on each doctrinal subject, trying to reduce each to its simplest terms and yet be able to cover all the most important doctrinal points in the available time.

The Principles is arranged into thirty-five lessons to be taught daily (five class periods a week) for the full twenty-six weeks. When the course is finished, the student should be able to intelligently discuss all the major Bible doctrines. The depth of teaching necessary depends entirely on the level of the class you are teaching. Depending on your class, there are some points of doctrine which may be reviewed very quickly.

If you are using our book, don't try to read aloud every single verse given as a reference. There are too many. For some doctrinal points, you might read one or two aloud. For others, you might even just refer to the references in passing. On critical points of doctrine, however, you must take more time, read several related verses (sometimes all of them), and emphasize the same point in several different ways so that it takes root and remains.

The Life and Teachings of Christ

The very first thing that Jesus did for us was to give us His example. First-century disciples adopted Christ's example so clearly that they were called *Christians.* Today, in the closing years of the twentieth century, we are called *Christians* also, but are we Christ-like? What could be more important than a study of His life?

There are various ways to study the life of Christ. It can be done chronologically, for example, or by subject. Personally, I love to study the miraculous aspects of the life of Christ. In our course, **The Life of Christ**, the miraculous aspects of His life are seen — as they relate to the fulfillment of prophecy. This first study is done as a basis for remembering His promise to us, *greater works than these shall ye do because I go unto my Father* (John 14:12). Such a study does two things for me: (1) It confirms to me WHO HE IS and (2) It shows me WHAT I CAN BE IN HIM.

In the same way, a great variety of teaching can be given under the title, **The Teachings of Christ**.

What did Jesus teach? And how did He teach it? In answering these questions, many approaches are taken. Most studies of Christ's teachings are based on the

Parables. While the Parables are important and rewarding to study, the real foundation stones of Christ's teachings are found in *The Sermon on the Mount*. There He teaches us not technique or method, but Christian principle and Christian character. If our students can develop the character of Jesus, so carefully laid out in *The Sermon on the Mount*, other important elements of ministry will fall into place for them.

Our study of **The Teachings of Christ** is based on *The Sermon on the Mount* as it is recorded in Matthew chapters six, seven and eight. The entire course is organized into forty-nine lessons that may be taught in twenty weeks.

Some of the teachings of Christ overlap — such as Mercy and Forgiveness, Humility and Meekness, Peacemakers and Reconciliation. We have attempted, in our own materials, not to repeat the same teaching over and over. The teacher must decide when to skip over some material that seems to be repetitious.

By combining the study of the miraculous aspects of Jesus' life with the character development of His most important sermon, we can accomplish a lot in a very short time. This, then, is our purpose.

Although the students will spend a lifetime deepening further their knowledge of Christ and His teachings, after twenty weeks they will have a general picture of both.

Prayer

If we can learn to pray effectively, everything else is possible to us. Successful prayer, however, is not automatic to the believer. Not every Christian knows how to

The Right Subject Matter

pray effectively. Many pray selfishly or against God's will. Successful prayer is not a technique but an attitude.

A thorough study of prayer, based, for the most part, on *The Lord's Prayer*, is organized into sixteen lessons that can be taught daily for one month.

As the lessons are applied daily in the prayer times, the students will become effective prayer warriors. Guided by the teachings of *The Lord's Prayer*, they will develop attitudes that enable them to successfully lay claim to God's promises.

Allowing one month for the study gives time for reviews, exams, and question-and-answer periods, as well.

Faith

Faith is both imparted and learned, and we utilize both methods.

This course on **Faith** is based on Hebrews, chapter eleven. Here the Bible holds up, as examples of faith, men and women of ancient biblical history. By studying in detail the lives of these heroes of faith, the students see that these men and women of old were just as human as we are. In the process, the students' faith begins to grow, faith that God can do for them the same miracles He did for the ancients — if they believe Him in the same way the ancients did. Hindrances to faith are also removed, as this subject is taught.

Learning about the Bible characters is not knowledge for knowledge sake. Well-taught, the course can be a means of inspiring God's trainees to great deeds of faith. Since everything we receive from God comes by faith, all of us need more of it, and no study could be more important.

The study is organized into eighteen lessons that may be taught in four to five weeks.

If you are unable to complete the eighteen lessons in the allotted time, it's okay. The major principles will have been learned, and the students may study the other lessons later, on their own time.

The Acts of the Apostles

This amazing portion of the Holy Scriptures is our handbook for world evangelization, our pattern book for church development, and we should study it verse by verse, placing emphasis on those teachings that will prepare the servant of God. The purpose of the study is to establish developing patterns in the scriptural history of the early church, patterns that we would want to repeat in our own lives.

We could separate each subject and develop it from the teachings of Acts on a page by itself. Baptism, for example, could be taught from chapters 2, 8, 9, 10, 16, 18, 19 and 22. But that is the approach taken in a study of doctrine. In this class, we prefer to see doctrines in action, the life of faith being lived. We want to see each subject in context. Some of the patterns of truth that we see developing deal with doctrinal issues and confirm what has been learned in **The Principles** class. But more often the patterns deal with very practical issues of the ministry.

As a pattern develops, it may not be necessary to spend the same amount of time with it the second time or the third time it is mentioned. It may be enough to note its presence, saying, for example, *"As we have noticed in earlier chapters, ..."* For that reason, in our study of **The Acts of the Apostles**, we simply propose things to *NOTE*.

As with other subjects, much time must be spent on some points, while others can simply be mentioned in passing, depending on the level of development of the group being taught. But don't take anything for granted. Make sure that your group has a solid foundation. Every pattern noted is important in the development of a well-rounded Christian life and ministry.

The *FOR THOUGHT* sections at the end of each of our chapters do not necessarily have a specific biblical answer. Your opinion on them may differ from others. The important thing is to ponder some of the mysterious aspects of the Scriptures.

The subject **Acts of the Apostles** is organized into twenty-nine lessons and cannot be finished in the eight weeks allotted. The major principles, however, repeated chapter by chapter, will have been learned. Go as far as you can, and the students may later complete the study on their own time.

Aside from those five basic subjects, I find the following subjects to be helpful when taught in a short-term course:

Bible Survey

While it is impossible to study the whole Bible in a twenty-six week period (as it is in a twenty-six year period) it is important to know something about each book of the Bible — the author, where and to whom the book was written, the principal theme of the book, the principal characters of the book and, perhaps, a key verse.

Since there are sixty-six books and only one hundred and twenty teaching periods dedicated to this subject, only one class period may be used for most of the smaller books. Two or three class periods may be used for the larger ones.

As some books are studied in detail during the course (the Gospels, The Acts of the Apostles, Romans, Daniel, The Revelation, etc.) these books may be skipped over in a Bible Survey course and that time dedicated to others.

When the twenty-six weeks have ended, the student will have a general knowledge of every book in the Bible.

Signs of the Coming of Christ

Knowledge of the Lord's coming is the strongest motivating force for evangelism. Of particular interest to us are the visible signs of His coming and their actual fulfillment all around us.

Following **The Life and Teachings of Christ**, two weeks of daily class periods will be dedicated solely to an inspired review of these signs and their significance to us as servants of God.

The History of the Church

A short study of **The History of the Church** should begin where **The Acts of the Apostles** ends and give the

The Right Subject Matter

highlights of the Church's history until the present day. Good books on the subject are recommended to the students for their own further and more detailed study.

Not all students will be able to absorb dozens of names and dates in a short time. Therefore, outlines, with dates and names are provided and a spiritual approach is taken to the subject, emphasizing such things as: evangelism, church growth, and resistance to persecution. Six weeks are available for this subject.

Modern Israel

The student who does not understand Israel's place in God's timetable — past, present and future — will never understand Bible prophecy. Under the theme Modern Israel we present a brief history of the Jewish people, beginning with the destruction of Jerusalem in 70 A.D. to the present, with major emphasis on the events leading up to and culminating in the founding of the nation of Israel and her miraculous survival since. Four weeks of daily sessions are allotted for the course.

Geography

The commission of Christ to the Church is: *Go ye into all the world.* Those who accept that commission and have a genuine burden for the world should begin to discover its peoples, their boundaries, their governments, their religions and their needs.

The subject is organized to alternate with **Language Improvement** during the entire twenty-six week period.

If **Geography** is needed more than **Language Improvement**, you may give it three class periods a week. If **Language Improvement** is needed more, give **Geography** only two periods a week.

Language Improvement

How can we communicate well the Gospel message if people cannot understand us? This class alternates with **Geography** during the entire twenty-six week period, and it includes oral presentations, reading assigned books and giving a written and/or oral report on what has been read.

On the basis of the difficulties encountered in both spoken and written language, the teacher will then present reviews of language structure, spelling and vocabulary.

Other Religions and False Cults

Here we must present a concise study of the other major religions and the major false cults of our times — their origins, their basic beliefs, their leaders, and their influence. The emphasis should be on how to win these people to Christ. Four weeks of daily class periods are allotted for the subject.

Evangelism (Soul-Winning)

What does the Bible say about evangelism? What techniques have been used successfully by the great evangelists of our time in mass evangelism, personal evangelism, child evangelism? Four weeks are allotted to learn effective biblical methods for systematic soul-winning.

Daniel and Revelation

A lifetime can be spent studying these two glorious books. The highlights can be reviewed in four weeks of daily class periods.

Music

Music is the language of the soul and plays a big part in the ministry. Since the class periods are all filled, a study of music must be done during two free evenings each week. Since the students have a long day, it is not good to teach heavy material at night. Music, however, is light and enjoyable.

The first weeks should be spent in music theory. Those students who are more advanced in music theory can help the others.

After theory, some time may be spent on voice. Here we should work with song leading (worship), choosing the proper key, beginning with the instruments, etc.

Then, divide the students into interest groups, and, during the last months, work (individually and with small groups) on voice and particular instruments, such as accordion and guitar (and/or piano and organ, when they are available).

Since the daily schedule of the training center is so heavy, practice time on musical instruments, except for the two evening periods, should be voluntary, and students may advance at their own pace.

Open Times

In the schedule we have presented here, sixteen weeks of one period daily are left open for subjects needed in your particular area. Those subjects might include, among others:

Leadership and Christian Ethics
Pastoral Studies
Literature Ministry
Drug Rehabilitation

These might also represent specialized studies for smaller groups, if desired. In that case, you would divide the students into small groups, depending on their interest or calling and dedicate special time with them in their chosen areas of study.

Concerning the materials we have prepared or those you might find elsewhere, each individual will disagree with some point of the prepared teachings. That is to be expected. I have never found anyone that I agreed with one hundred percent, and no one has to agree with me on every single point of doctrine to be blessed of God or to go to Heaven. The Church of the Lord Jesus Christ is made up of many parts and represents unity in diversity. We are all serving the same God and working toward the same end — despite our differences of viewpoint!

The Right Subject Matter

Sometimes our differences are only a question of semantics or the way a thought is expressed. If it is a minor point that does not hinder spiritual development, I ignore it, and you should do the same. If, however, it is (or seems to be) a serious point of Bible doctrine, you may have to eliminate that material from your course. Take what you can from existing materials and adapt them to your own needs. The important thing is to get started *Laying Biblical Foundations.*

A Sample Schedule of Subjects

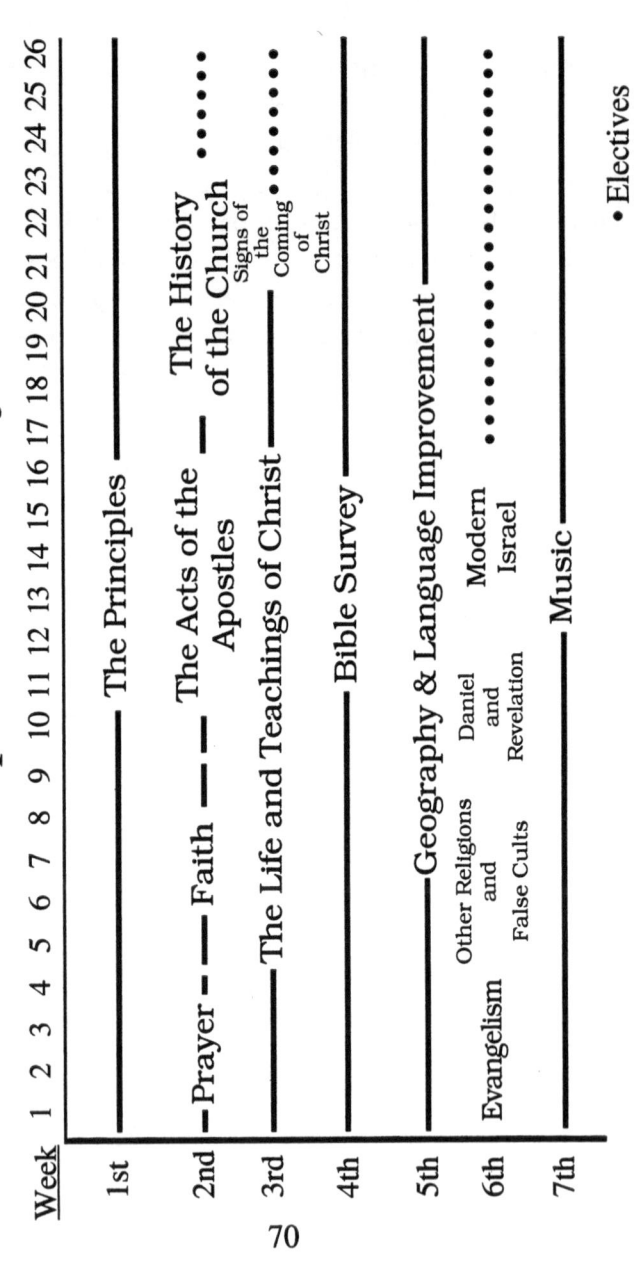

Week	1 2 3 4 5 6 7 8 9 10 11 12 13 14 15 16 17 18 19 20 21 22 23 24 25 26
1st	———————— The Principles ————————
2nd	— Prayer — — Faith — — The Acts of the Apostles — — The History of the Church ••••••••
3rd	———— The Life and Teachings of Christ ———— Signs of the Coming of Christ ••••••••
4th	———————— Bible Survey ————————
5th	———————— Geography & Language Improvement ————————
6th	Evangelism / Other Religions and False Cults / Daniel and Revelation / Modern Israel ••••••••••••••••••
7th	———————— Music ———————— • Electives

- 13 -

LAYING BIBLICAL FOUNDATIONS
The Use of the Book Principles of Christian Faith

The materials that we have prepared for the first five subjects we teach in an intensive short-term course of preparation are printed in textbook form in the volume entitled: ***Principles of Christian Faith, Volume I.*** This book was developed over a period of twenty years through my own teaching in Bible schools in Asia, Latin America and Africa, and that gives it several great advantages:

1. **It is trans-cultural**, that is, its teachings apply to people in a variety of cultural settings.

2. **It is simple.** In order to minister to people who have English as a second language, ***Principles of***

Christian Faith uses only 1,200 unique English words.

3. **It is organized and formatted for classroom use.** Recognizing the leadership crisis in every major Christian field of endeavor and the need to quickly train sincere men and women for the harvest, I designed the book to provide a ready-made system of doing just that. It is used effectively in training centers in many parts of the world.

Principles of Christian Faith is being used similarly in home and church Bible study groups, and even as a guide for special Sunday school studies. Prison ministry groups find it to be exactly what they need to lay practical foundations in the men and women to whom they minister on a regular basis.

The book also has many uses outside of the formal Bible study setting.

1. *Principles of Christian Faith* is useful **as resource material**. Since the book covers all the major Christian doctrines in the section **The Principles, The Life and Teachings of Christ, Prayer, Faith** and the history of their early use in **The Acts of the Apostles,** it is a valuable source of information for pastors, Sunday school teachers, and youth leaders. The various indexes help to locate material on a broad range of subjects.

2. *Principles of Christian Faith* is useful **as a personal guide to study** for those who feel the need

Use of the Book *Principles of Christian Faith*

to prepare themselves in any area of Christian fundamentals. For example, pastors, before preaching on a particular subject, find it useful to review all the biblical teaching on that subject.

3. Although *Principles of Christian Faith* is not recommended for casual reading, many find it useful **as a means of refreshing the memory** on basic Christian principles.

4. A studious and disciplined person will find *Principles of Christian Faith* to be useful **as a complete Home Study Bible School Course**.

5. *Principles of Christian Faith* may effectively be used **as a guide to teach children** of all ages the basic tenets of our faith.

Whatever your emphasis, this book is especially designed to help you in *Laying Biblical Foundations*.

- 14 -

LAYING BIBLICAL FOUNDATIONS
The Use of Prepared Teaching Materials

In a college-level class, materials are made available to the student, and he digs the information out for himself. The professor leads class discussions and keeps things on track. In the Bible school short-term course, there is no time for that approach. It would take students years to "dig out" what an anointed teacher can give them in a few moments.

For many years, as I was developing and using the short-term course, I never provided any written materials for the student. I wanted his/her full attention. Later, I began to prepare simple outlines to place in the hands of the students, and I found it very helpful for several reasons:

The Use of Prepared Teaching Materials

1. If I put a simple outline in the students' hands, then they don't have to make copious notes of their own as I speak. They can give their full attention to what I am teaching.

2. The students may make additional notes or clarifications on the same outline — if they wish to do so.

3. The students may review the material periodically, at their leisure.

4. Until they become gifted in teaching (and for those who never develop a gift for organizing material systematically), students may use the material to teach others. [This always presents a danger of dependence on the materials instead of seeking God for a message or for a gift of teaching, and we must warn against this danger.]

If you can make some prepared outlines available to those you are teaching, it may be helpful in *Laying Biblical Foundations.*

- 15 -

LAYING BIBLICAL FOUNDATIONS
Rules and Regulations For the Course

You must have rules for your Bible training program. These rules should be thoroughly explained during the initial week of activities and should be strictly enforced. Although rules may vary from place to place, the following general rules are considered essential:

THE STUDENT SHALL:

- *Maintain a pleasant spirit at all times*

- *Maintain an acceptable academic average in his/her studies*

The Use of Prepared Teaching Materials

- *Maintain an acceptable spiritual level*

- *Maintain himself, his clothing, his room, and his other surroundings clean and neat at all times*

- *Be properly dressed at all times (local standards will define proper dress)*

- *Attend and be on time for all prayer times, classes, work periods, meals and services*

- *Respect teachers, pastors, the members of the church and fellow students*

- *Perform cheerfully all assigned tasks*

- *Not leave the premises without permission*

- *Refrain from courting during the course of training*

Other rules may be added, as needed, as you continue *Laying Biblical Foundations.*

- 16 -

LAYING BIBLICAL FOUNDATIONS
Beginning

How to begin? Many people have a burden to prepare laborers for the harvest, but they don't know how to begin.

While you can't expect to have everything perfectly organized before you begin, you basically need six things to get started:

You Need Ministers

First, you need ministers — a director and some teachers. There can be no ministry without qualified ministers. Ask God to reveal to you those in your midst who are capable of teaching. Then ask those individuals if they would be willing to accept the responsibility of teaching.

Beginning

Don't be discouraged if some refuse. The Lord will show you others who can replace any who are unwilling or unable to serve in this capacity. (See *The Right Director*, page 47 and *The Right Teachers*, page 49.)

You Need A Date

Next, you need a date to work toward. This date could be as little as four to six weeks away or as much as several months away. In the more developed countries we tend to schedule things much further in advance than in the lesser developed countries.

The important thing is not to wait too long. Set a date for the initial interviews for prospective students and the opening date for classes (in the developing countries we set the opening date for one week after the interviews).

Allow enough time for those who need to give advance notice for leaving a job. If you have a major campaign or a camp meeting, begin soon after it ends in order to take advantage of the fruit of that meeting.

You Need Students

You need students, and you can get them through your own church and outreach ministry activities. Crusades and camp meetings are ideal recruitment centers. When you preach, believe God to raise up the workers you need.

When we preach, believing for souls to be saved, we see souls coming to Christ. When we preach, believing for those who are sick to be healed, wonderful miracles take place. When we preach, believing for men and women to be filled with the Holy Spirit, we experience an outpouring of the Spirit upon those who hear us. Use your faith in the same way for prospective workers. If you need workers, believe that as you minister God will call young men and women to His harvest field. He will not fail you.

Announce the upcoming training sessions in all your own churches, crusades, outstations, and street meetings. You will usually be surprised how many will want to attend.

You can also get students by sending people out to announce the course in other cities (depending on the size of the country), in other churches, in campaigns, ministers' conferences, campmeetings, etc.

Print or mimeograph an information sheet that contains the most important information about the course:

- *Twenty-six weeks of classroom training*

- *Twenty-six weeks of field training*

- *Spirit-filled teachers*

- *The cost (if the program is free, indicate that)*

- *The starting date_____*

- *Students must appear on (<u>the date</u>) for personal interviews*

- *The address (for responses)*

- *The sponsoring church, etc.*

Let this information sheet be widely distributed, and many will respond. In a later section, we will discuss how to choose the type of students you need from those who do respond.

You Need A Location

You need a location. If necessary, make some quick adjustments to your existing facility. You can improve it slowly as the course progresses. (See *The Right Facilities*, page 43.)

You Need A Program

You do need a program, but we have provided a sample program here. You may simply choose to follow our program, at least until you have developed one of your own, one that addresses your own particular needs. If you use our program, don't hesitate to adjust it to your own circumstances.

You Need Subject Matter

The final thing you need is the subject matter you will teach. We have outlined here what we use. (See *The Right Subject Matter*, page 57, and *The Appendix*.)

Some materials must be developed, as needed, by individual teachers, but, don't wait for your teachers to develop their materials before you begin. Begin NOW!

Don't postpone the opening of your training session for six months to renovate the building, to prepare more teachers or more materials. Begin! It's harvest time.

As a youth I learned that compelling chorus of harvest, which I still believe:

> *Harvest time*
> *Harvest time*
> *The grain is falling.*
> *The Savior's calling.*
> *Oh, do not wait.*
> *It's growing late.*
> *Lift up your eyes.*
> *Behold, it's harvest time.*
>
> — Author unknown

Act now to begin *Laying Biblical Foundations.*

- 17 -

LAYING BIBLICAL FOUNDATIONS
The Screening of Students

The selection of the students for an intensive short-term Bible training program is as important, or possibly more so, than anything else about the course. So, although I have mentioned it already, I give it additional space here.

Set a date for student interviews. Include an early morning beginning time, or many will arrive too late. Begin the morning with prayer, some worship, and an anointed message about the seriousness of the call of God and the purpose of the course.

Have a simple application form ready that the applicants can fill out sometime during the morning or you may have them send it in ahead of time so that you could be studying it. You might want the application to contain:

- *Name?*

- *Address?*

- *Age?*

- *Marital status?*

- *Number of children?*

- *Educational attainment?*

- *Other training?*

- *Profession?*

- *Church affiliation?*

- *Born again?*

- *Baptized in water?*

- *Baptized in the Holy Ghost?*

- *Calling?*

- *Previous Bible training?*

Here are some other questions that we have also found to be very helpful in this regard:

The Screening of Students

- *If you are married: Is your companion a Christian and in agreement with your entering the training?*

- *If you still live at home: Are your parents in agreement?*

- *If you are from another church: Is your pastor in agreement?*

- *Do you agree with the doctrinal position of the school? (The doctrinal position can appear on the reverse of the form.)*

- *Do you have outstanding debts?*

- *Have you ever been convicted of a crime?*

- *Have you ever suffered a contagious disease?*

- *Are you willing to abide by all the rules of the course? (These can be posted or a copy provided to each prospective student so that everyone reads them during the morning.)*

When the applications are returned to you, retire to a private place and begin reviewing them, underlining in red anything that might present a problem or that needs to be clarified or otherwise called to the attention of other interviewers.

After lunch and a rest time, have someone else continue with the applicants in a service similar to the morning's, while you receive the students one by one for a personal interview. Have someone act as a runner to call the students in turn. While they are coming, read off the most important points of the application to the whole group (I suggest a group of three or four interviewers). The time you can spend with each applicant may depend on how many applicants there are and how much time you have available.

With the information from the application as a background, begin to ask important questions that will help you make a proper decision concerning each one. Each of the several interviewers should, without comment to the others, make an immediate note on his list of prospective students. This classification of candidates noted by each interviewer might be as follows:

1. *Accept without reservation*
2. *Accept with reservation*
3. *Not sure*
4. *Reject with reservation*
5. *Reject without reservation*

Then continue with the next candidate. Later, when all the applicants have had an initial interview, you can begin to make your choices.

When all the interviewers agree to accept an applicant without reservation or to reject an applicant without reservation, those decisions are easy. When there is no agreement, or you are not sure what the correct decision is, you may want to call the applicant back for a few more minutes of questioning to clarify any doubts.

When your final decisions have been made and before

a list of those accepted is made public, you need to call, one by one, those who are rejected and personally explain to them why they were not accepted. Be frank. Tell them if they are too young, too immature or have a marriage complication. For some, the timing is just not right. Encourage and admonish each one to seek God and overcome their limitations, work with their own pastor or come back next time when they have settled debts or otherwise removed the obstacles to serious preparation for the ministry. A rejection can be devastating in some countries. Do it with great wisdom and love and always give hope for the future.

Call those who are accepted with reservation and explain to them that, for this or that reason, they are provisionally accepted, but that their progress during the week of prayer may determine if they will stay on or not. This will challenge them to make an extra effort and will make it easier for you to dismiss them, if that should become necessary, during the early weeks.

Before the day ends, give those who have been accepted an idea of the type of clothing and other personal items they will need to bring with them when they return for the opening of classes.

Accept latecomers (those who come days later) only in special cases. As a rule, do not accept more applicants after the week of prayer. At that point, new applicants are already too far behind to be able to catch up to the others. You are making progress toward *Laying Biblical Foundations.*

- 18 -

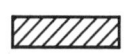

LAYING BIBLICAL FOUNDATIONS
The Week of Prayer

We find it especially helpful to begin a short-term Bible training program with an entire week of intensive prayer. Several things are accomplished by this:

1. A week of prayer gives any student who is not Spirit-filled an opportunity to receive the baptism of the Holy Ghost before continuing. This is extremely important. Those who are not Spirit-filled will not do well in the course. Letting them know that they are only provisionally accepted, because of this limitation, will give them an added incentive to seek God wholeheartedly during the prayer times.

The Week of Prayer

2. A week of prayer allows a few more days to observe and pray with those students who are conditionally accepted, but who may not stay on for various reasons — such as a bad attitude or incompatible doctrinal positions.

3. A week of prayer gives any ill students the opportunity to be healed so that they will not be hindered during the teaching periods by their physical condition. Leaders can give teachings that will enable students to maintain their healing and to remain healthy throughout the course.

4. A week of prayer will lift the students into the proper spiritual atmosphere to begin their studies and will enable them to clear their minds of their former surroundings and circumstances.

5. A week of prayer allows the student time to adjust to his new surroundings and his new companions.

6. A week of prayer gives time for any special preliminary instruction and an opportunity to explain the rules and regulations of the center, the schedules, and the subjects, etc.

7. A week of prayer also gives the teachers and other spiritual leaders in the training center the opportunity to move into a new place in God and to prepare themselves for the challenge of mold-

ing the lives entrusted to them into vessels pleasing to the Lord.

During this week of prayer, a precedent must be set for the spiritual atmosphere of the course. Since the students must be lifted up into a new realm in the Spirit, it is the responsibility of those in charge to lead the way.

During that week, pray with individual students, taking authority over anything that might hinder them in the coming days and weeks and helping them to begin their training free of such hindrances, whatever they might be. Teach them to take authority themselves and to do battle with the enemy of their souls on a regular basis.

Help the students to cast off grudges from the past and to free themselves of all unforgiveness and malice towards others, whoever they might be. Teach them the importance of clearing the air so that they can prosper spiritually and put their minds and hearts to the task ahead.

Instruct the students concerning praying in the Spirit, and singing in the Spirit and let those who are in charge set the example for others to follow.

A typical schedule for the week of prayer might look like this:

7:30	A.M.	Prayer
8:30	A.M.	Service, with prayer to continue through the morning
12:00	Noon	Noon Meal
1:00	P.M.	Rest

The Week of Prayer

    2:30 P.M.   Prayer
    3:00 P.M.   Service with prayer continuing through the afternoon
                    Evening Service or instruction

It is helpful to have the graduates of former classes participate in this week of prayer. They can help pray for the new ones, lead the worship, give testimonies and preach. There should be very special messages of deep consecration.

The first fast day should be observed this week. On occasion, as the Lord leads, even two or three days of fasting can be observed during the week of prayer. Everyone will benefit from the fasting, spiritually and even physically.

The most important thing to accomplish during this week of prayer is to touch Heaven and get God's touch on the teachers, the students, and the program. You are now getting down to serious business, the business of ***Laying Biblical Foundations.***

- 19 -

LAYING BIBLICAL FOUNDATIONS
The Daily Schedule

Once you have ended the week of prayer, you will want to enter into an established daily routine. The daily schedule for an intensive short-term Bible training course must be adapted to local conditions and customs. The following is a schedule that has proven very effective:

Morning

      7:00 A.M. Breakfast
      7:30 A.M. Prayer
      8:30 A.M. Meditation
      9:00 A.M. First Class Period

The Daily Schedule

9:45 A.M.	Break
10:00 A.M.	Second Class Period
10:45 A.M.	Third Class Period
12:00 Noon	Noon Meal

Afternoon

1:00 P.M.	Rest
2:30 P.M.	Prayer and Memorization
3:00 P.M.	Fourth Class Period
3:45 P.M.	Fifth Class Period
4:30 P.M.	Break
4:45 P.M.	Sixth Class Period

Evening

| 6:00 P.M. | Evening Meal |
| 7:30 P.M. | Evening Service Seventh Class Period or Study Time |

This schedule was developed with the following experiences in mind:

Very early rising is a good habit for the servant of God to develop. However, the schedule of such a course is so heavy that the students must get proper rest. Loud singing in the dormitories during afternoon rest time, night time or early morning hours cannot be permitted. A student who is accustomed to rising extremely early to pray and sing in a loud voice might go to the chapel to avoid disturbing others.

Although it is good to have prayer before breakfast, I prefer going directly into the teaching after morning prayer and not losing the anointing by breaking for breakfast. So I suggest going right through the morning with only one fifteen minute break.

The thirty minutes following the prayer is for some worship and a short message of inspiration for the day. During the first months, the pastor, teachers, and visiting speakers will give these messages. In the later months, the students, themselves, will do it.

The Psalms can also be read here, but remember, the time is short.

On special days or weeks, the schedule can be pushed aside to make room for a visiting minister. In these cases, you will want to have more of a service with time for personal ministry. But, if you do this every day, you cannot possibly cover the foundation material in the few months of the course. On normal days, try to stick to the schedule as much as possible.

Each class time is set at forty-five minutes. Personally, I prefer an hour, but I find that if you cut each class to forty-five minutes and change the theme each class period, the students do not tire as easily, and they learn more.

Although only fifteen minutes break is given, students are free at any time to step out to the rest room and to get a drink. The class continues, so they should come back as quickly as possible.

Although work will be assigned to the students in the course of the training program, it is not convenient to take them out of class to run errands or cook. At the close

The Daily Schedule

of their morning classes, some may help serve the tables, while others wash their clothes and others simply relax in preparation for the meal.

The meals should be served as much on time as possible. If the noon meal is served late, the students will lose their rest time. If the evening meal is late, they will be late for service.

The two-thirty prayer time gives a good start on the afternoon and allows ten to fifteen minutes to review the memory verse for that day and those of former days, as well.

Then, there are three more class periods of forty-five minutes each before the evening meal.

When there are no evening services scheduled, some light classes can be conducted or students can be given study periods.

Lights out time should be set at a fair hour, depending on when the services generally end.

On fast days, the schedule can be the same, except the meal times are eliminated. Some students will want to pray together during the skipped meal time, but this should be voluntary.

Short periods of recreation can be scheduled for free evenings, Saturdays, or during times when students are waiting for meals or for other activities to begin.

This is all part of the exciting and rewarding process of *Laying Biblical Foundations.*

- 20 -

LAYING BIBLICAL FOUNDATIONS
Preparation For the Classroom

The first and most important element of preparation for those who will teach an intensive short-term Bible course, is not preparing a lesson or even a subject but preparing themselves. If your own life is not in order, the best materials presented in the very best way will fail to produce fruit.

On the other hand, failure to prepare well for the particular lesson you are called upon to teach is also unacceptable. The students must sit there for many hours, day after day. If they hear the same thing over and over, who could blame them if they grow weary of it? Students for the ministry need a wide variety of teaching, a full foundation for their ministries.

Preparation For the Classroom

Each teacher must develop his/her own method of preparation for the classroom. Some teachers need to begin preparing weeks in advance. Others need to have the material fresh. A good practice is to combine these two methods. Prepare yourself as far ahead as possible. Then, review the material a day or so before the class period so that it will be fresh in your spirit.

Being well prepared means knowing the material you will teach. If you have taught the subject on other occasions you may feel comfortable teaching it again with only last-minute review. If, however, you have never taught the subject, or if you wish to teach it in a different way, you may want to do the following:

- Read over any material available (such as the outlines we provide).

- Read the related verses from the Bible.

- If you are reading from the Gospels, read the same story in each of the Gospels in which it is recorded. Each will give you a few more details and another perspective of the same teaching or story.

- If a New Testament verse is the fulfillment of an Old Testament verse, or at least refers to an Old Testament verse, read the Old Testament verse also.

- If you read in any other languages, read the same verse in another language.

- As you read, mark things on your study outline that you want to emphasize. Mark verses that you want to read aloud or have the students read aloud.

- Make a note also of words you do not understand very well, verses you do not understand well, and teachings you do not understand well. Students may ask you about these points, so don't just skip over them. Look those subjects up and pray about them, seeking understanding.

Sometimes a Bible dictionary may help you to understand Bible words; but be cautious. Bible dictionaries are not infallible.

Many study Bibles (and there are some good ones) give a brief explanation of a difficult word in the marginal notes. These can be very helpful; but, again, be cautious. The margin notes in study Bibles are not infallible.

Because the Word of God is infallible, use your concordance to look up a word you have difficulty understanding. Jot down a few verses in which it is used. Read those verses. Although you will note that words are often used differently in the Old Testament and in the New, you will generally get a good idea of the meaning of the word in question simply by reading the Bible — especially if you can read it in two or more languages

Preparation For the Classroom

(not Greek and Hebrew, but modern languages you read and speak).

Concerning the use of Bible commentaries for preparing yourself, first I would say don't read commentaries at all when you're young. Your own beliefs are not yet well formed, and you tend to accept everything you read. Many commentarists were not spirit-filled men and their insight into our present time was limited. Although they wrote with deep sincerity, their writings may have limited value for us today.

When you are more mature, use a commentary as a last resort on difficult matters, and don't feel robbed if you find you don't have access to one. Commentarists do not agree on the difficult issues of the Christian faith. You might study all the great commentaries and still not understand many Bible passages.

- Whatever you read, do it prayerfully, asking the Lord to give you wisdom. Always remember that He promised wisdom to those who ask Him.

- Talk over problematic words and verses with mature believers whom you respect. They may have some insight that can help you.

- Although you want to prepare well, don't be overly concerned about obscure points of doctrine. There is too much to be done for us to sit around and take the spiritual luxury of arguing the various viewpoints about this or that passage. If something you don't understand affects your daily life, ask the Lord what He wants you to do about it. If an obscure point does not affect your daily life, forget it. If it was so important, the Lord would have explained it more simply in His Word.

All the major doctrines are plainly outlined again and again in the Bible. The fact that something is not clearly outlined, therefore, seems to me to mean that God did not think it was vitally important for you to understand. Tell your students the same thing when they ask you about those obscure passages.

- Before class time, be sure that physical preparation is also made. Did you want to distribute some maps of Israel? Did you want to post a chart on the board? For those who use chalk, is it available? There is nothing worse than sitting in a classroom while a teacher hunts for an eraser or a piece of chalk.

- Lastly, perhaps the most important thing you can do to prepare for teaching others is to get inspired. It might happen weeks before a class. It might happen in your sleep the night before. Or, it might happen while you are standing before the students. But let God inspire and enlighten you.

Teach as the prophets of old, giving forth the needed Word to those who are before you and not a warmed-over teaching that was for people in another time and situation.

Get excited about the divine prospect of *Laying Biblical Foundations.*

- 21 -

LAYING BIBLICAL FOUNDATIONS
Testing

In an intensive short-term course of Bible training, we are not interested in testing for the same reasons a secular school uses testing. Testing in the secular sense reveals very little about spiritual progress. Those who are quick to memorize and quick to understand and remember are not always those who make the best servants of God. Often, a seemingly poor student will persevere and become an excellent minister.

Testing, however, does serve several useful purposes for us:

- Testing reveals problem areas in the group as a whole and in individuals in particular. We can then deal with those specific problems.

Testing

- Testing reveals whether or not a student is listening well or simply daydreaming.

- Testing challenges a student to do his/her very best.

- Testing helps a teacher to know if he or she is adequately covering the truth of the subject at hand.

Because there is so much material to cover in a limited time in a short course, tests should be few and simple. We should never ask the students, for example, for obscure dates or names. Each test should cover important principles and spiritual truths, and nothing more.

There are several ways of testing. At least once, at the beginning of the course, I like to tell (or even read aloud) some Bible story. Then, without warning, I give a test on what I have read with a few choice questions from the story. This alerts the students to the fact that they must always listen carefully to the teaching we are giving them.

During the course, I give at least one other surprise test. Upon entering the classroom, I begin the class as usual and then announce that we will have a question and answer period (I will ask the questions, and they will give the answers — on paper). I may not give another surprise test the entire course, but the students will always be ready.

For subjects that occupy four to eight weeks, one exam can be given with several days or a week of advance notice. Allow one class period to finish the exam. I always allow those who finish early to have the remainder of the class period free.

While grading the tests, if you notice that all or most of the students missed a certain question, check to see if you worded that question poorly. We all do it sometimes. Explain your error to the class and given them credit for one correct answer.

Finish grading the tests as soon as possible and return them to the students while the material is still fresh in their minds. Then, take a class period or two to review the test material, recognizing those who did well on the exam, without embarrassing those who did poorly.

Later, one by one, send for those who did not do well on the test and have a personal talk with them. If necessary, use a tone of firmness. Warn them that they simply must improve their grades. Since the course covers basics, each student should be expected to maintain a seventy per cent average.

But be merciful when mercy is called for. Consider the educational background of the student and any other complicating factors. Often, a show of compassion is needed at this point. Take time to pray with a failing student. Help him to clear his mind of hindrances, family problems, romance, financial problems, and spiritual instability or immaturity. Dismissal for a failure on exams should be a last resort.

Most importantly, encourage students who are not doing well on exams that they can do better, and expect them to do better from that day forward.

When a subject continues for longer than six or eight weeks or even the entire twenty-six week period, several exams may be needed at intervals of six to eight weeks. We feel that each teacher is capable of making that decision and of preparing the exam itself.

We have prepared no standard exams to accompany the course we have developed. If we had them, they might fall into the hands of the students before exam time. So each teacher should make up his/her own exam shortly before the day it is given. Most people who are capable of teaching have the sense of the important things that need to be remembered from that teaching.

I believe that we should have zero tolerance for cheating on such exams, and I am very strict in this matter. Let your test be an opportunity to show that those who cheat in life lose in the end.

Testing serves a useful purpose in *Laying Biblical Foundations.*

- 22 -

LAYING BIBLICAL FOUNDATIONS
Outside Activities

During the first few months of the short-term course, the students should not be sent out for outside ministry. They should even be discouraged from visiting their homes on weekends. The weekend atmosphere and activity of the church is important to their early development.

Encourage students to write home once in a while (once a week would be good), to show respect for their parents, their pastors or any benefactors. Gratitude is an important lesson to be taught

Once the students begin to develop well, then they need to have opportunities for ministry. They may begin in the local church with a testimony or a special song and personal ministry to those who come forward for prayer

Outside Activities

in any particular service. After a few months, assign a teacher the responsibility of organizing street ministry. The street is the best place for the student to begin his ministry. He has more now than the average person on the street. He has something to offer. He may sing, testify, or preach and pray for the individuals who want to be saved and healed and ministered to.

In some countries, street preaching is prohibited and, in others, is ineffective. A substitute can be found. The students may minister in jails, in schools, in marketplaces, in homes for the elderly, in hospitals, in leper colonies — anywhere where people have a need and where the door is open to the Gospel.

Be sure that these outings are well organized and, at first, supervised. Do not expect the students to find their way blindly. They need your help to get started.

Be open from the beginning with the students with praise for a job well-done and a loving word of correction or an occasional rebuke, as needed.

Don't let these outside activities be long and drawn out at first. There are already many demands on the students' time.

Begin outside activities on a Saturday afternoon, or a Sunday afternoon between services. Later, outside ministry can be done several times a week, even occasionally taking an hour or two of class time.

As you give the students opportunity to participate in services, you will notice that some are especially gifted in song leading, special singing, preaching or even teaching. Be careful! It is wrong to give these more-gifted ones unlimited opportunity at the expense of other students.

Each one needs opportunity. If one is favored, several wrongs result:

1. There is always a danger of pride among young people when they are used of God, especially when they become more visible than others. If you notice pride developing in a student, let them sit for a while without participating. Pride is very dangerous to their further spiritual development.

2. Other students will become jealous of a classmate who is favored and bitter against the leaders who show such favoritism.

Students should not, during the training program, be placed as preachers in major services. This would not be good for them. Let them speak in the morning meditation, at young peoples' meetings, and in outside activities — nothing more, for now.

When the students go out for their outside activities, it is good for them to walk, if possible. After sitting for hours each day, a good walk will do them a world of good.

As you apply these timely principles, you are learning to be effective in *Laying Biblical Foundations*.

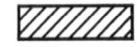

- 23 -

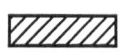

LAYING BIBLICAL FOUNDATIONS
Physical Work

The students in an intensive short-term training course need to have assigned chores, for several reasons:

1. They sit for hours each day, so they need physical activity. Cleaning, going to the market, carrying something, moving furniture, or similar activities that serve a practical purpose can provide that activity.

2. All students need to learn the dignity of work so they will not look down on common laborers, as people in many countries do.

3. Work is part of the personal discipline so necessary to the students' development.

4. Working helps the students to realize what the ministry is: "work" — not just singing and talking.

5. Work has a certain humbling effect.

The work that is assigned to the students of an intensive short-term course should be, as much as possible, group work. The reason is that the students must learn to work together with all their brothers and sisters.

Work, during the early months at least, should be closely supervised. You need to:

- See that everyone participates

- Teach the students how to develop good work habits

- Set an example to be emulated

- See that the conversation is wholesome

- See that the activity does not end in foolishness that destroys the spirit

- Detect any frictions among brothers and sisters

The students should keep the temple and its surroundings spotlessly clean and neat. They should wash all their

Physical Work

dishes and clean their tables. They can paint and do simple repairs to the facilities. And it is not wrong to occasionally take a day or two off and use the students for a worthy construction project. They will learn much, accomplish much, and enjoy the break from studies and the physical exercise it affords.

In our own training centers, we have always enjoyed doing some sort of project for the benefit of the community, such as cleaning, repairing, or painting some public building or facility. The students always benefit, and we leave a good testimony for the people of the neighborhood.

It's all part of *Laying Biblical Foundations.*

- 24 -

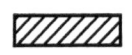

LAYING BIBLICAL FOUNDATIONS
Sports?

In our age of health consciousness, there is a cry to provide sports facilities for Bible school students. The Scriptures answer this way:

> *Bodily exercise profiteth little, but godliness is profitable unto all things, having promise of the life that now is, and of that which is to come.*
> 1 Timothy 4:8

Some people are lethargic in the morning. If they need to get out in the fresh air and do some exercises before breakfast, that is fine. But this cannot be required. Let it be voluntary.

Sports?

Beyond the need of some for some exercise to help them get started, a few moments of sports (such as basketball, volleyball, or football) would not harm the students and should be permitted, and even encouraged, during free time. Since their free time is limited, the danger hardly exists that these activities will become excessive — as they easily can.

At first, students should be supervised even at sports, to be sure that a good spirit is maintained.

Brisk walking should be done by the entire group when on the way to their outstations. Generally speaking, the students will get their exercise through assigned work.

These seem like insignificant points, but they all contribute to effectively *Laying Biblical Foundations.*

- 25 -

LAYING BIBLICAL FOUNDATIONS
The Final Week

The final week of the classroom training in an intensive short-term course should be both a time of celebration and of additional preparation. All of the associated ministers should be invited in for several days of special convention, with services in the morning, afternoon and evening. It is good to combine this week of special meetings with other church or Bible school activities, for instance, the graduation of a previous class. And the members of the church\es should attend, as well.

During this week of activity, the students should be encouraged to participate in any way possible in the services. During some services, you can have young ministers testify of their struggles and their victories.

The Final Week

Students will learn a lot from them.

During all the services, special prayer should be offered. But, in one very special service, perhaps the last, something should be said of the field assignments for the students. Then hands should be laid on each one of them, believing God for a new anointing for their lives, for the impartation of special gifts and ministries to them, and for any personal word the Lord might have for each one of them. In this way, the students are launched forth on a high note of victory and get a good start in the practical part of their training.

This celebration week is usually not the time for fasting, but rather for feasting, and when it is completed, you have taken another critical step in ***Laying Biblical Foundations.***

- 26 -

LAYING BIBLICAL FOUNDATIONS
The Field Training

The field training for the intensive short-term Bible training course should be more or less the same length as the classroom training. It is accomplished by organizing the students into small groups or teams that will each have an experienced pastor, evangelist, missionary or Christian worker as its leader. Most teams should not exceed four members, except in special circumstances, because larger teams are difficult for local people to house, feed and transport.

Each team should be assigned an area in which to work. As they work, the disciplines they have begun in their period of classroom training must continue.

The morning prayer times should continue, but the timing of the morning prayer may be decided by the

The Field Training

team, taking local needs into account.

The regular fasting should continue, although the team may be at liberty to decide when and how they fast.

The morning meditation should continue, given either by the team leader or a member that he or she chooses.

The personal disciplines should continue.

One hour and a half of study should be done daily on some correspondence course selected to meet the local needs. The study may be done at a time that will not conflict with the actual work assigned.

The work should be organized by the team leader and should consist of at least four hours daily of ministry in prisons, army bases, schools, houses, market places or just on the street. (See the next chapter: *The Plan for Evangelization.*)

In addition, the students should attend and participate in local services.

If the team is assigned to a large city, it could remain there for the entire twenty-six weeks. If their assignment is a small village, they might be moved regularly to give them new opportunities and to reach more people.

The team should have a good amount of literature on hand to use in its outreach:

- Tracts for street meetings

- Gospels to give to new converts

- Books and/or Bibles to present to school libraries, to city and state officials and to other important dignitaries

- Booklets about the Holy Ghost baptism and the signs of the Second Coming of Christ to give to church leaders

(For more details on the use of literature in this program, see *Materials For Evangelism*, page 127).

After three months of field work, all the teams should gather again at the training center, and several days should be spent together in reflection, prayer and exhortation. The team leaders should give reports, and everyone may testify during this time.

The team leaders may report privately some disciplinary problem that needs to be dealt with during these few days.

During those days, some adjustments may be needed in the size of teams, their leaders, or their assignments. Make these adjustments prayerfully.

While everyone is together, an exam should be given on the correspondence material studied over the past three months. Problems will surface. Warn any students who get behind in their studies that the correspondence course is part of the overall program of training and is needed for graduation. The idea is for the students to develop permanent study habits, even when they are away from the center.

Lay hands on everyone during a final service and commission them to another three months of reaping. Believe God for additional anointing for their assigned labor and for the impartation of spiritual gifts and ministries to each of them. Then, send the teams forth again.

During these weeks of field training, a record should

The Field Training

be kept daily by the team leader about the team's activities — the places visited, the preaching, the teaching, the testifying, how many responded, the literature distributed, etc. These reports will be periodically sent or taken to the training center, where they will be evaluated and then shared and published. This accomplishes several objectives:

- To give the students and leaders a sense of accountability

- To cement in the minds of everyone involved, the fruit that is resulting from the efforts being made

- To teach students the importance of expressing gratitude to the Lord, to financial supporters, etc.

In this way, you continue *Laying Biblical Foundations.*

- 27 -

LAYING BIBLICAL FOUNDATIONS
The Plan For Evangelization

The field training should be done under a specific plan. This is not to say that you must always use the same plan, or that the plan cannot, at some point, be modified to meet local conditions. But a plan is necessary, nevertheless.

If there are no specific goals, how will it be known later if the goals were achieved? If you do not outline exactly what you expect of the students, how will they know they are accomplishing anything, and how will you judge, later, their performance? The fact that spiritual progress is not easy to measure should never cause us to fall into the trap of not expecting our students to achieve specific goals.

The Plan For Evangelization

We cannot guarantee how many souls will be won, how many sick will be healed or how many men and women will be baptized in the Holy Ghost; but we can be sure that the Gospel is preached and the sick and hungry are ministered to. We do this through a systematic plan for evangelism. This is biblical.

The Apostles went to each town and village and preached. The time they spent in each place depended on the size of the place, the response they received to the ministry, and the time it took them to effectively enter each open door. It is with this biblical example in mind that we offer the following plan as a general guide:

Each team should be equipped with a small, battery-operated sound system, if possible, and should take on their initial journey as many boxes of tracts, Gospels, Bibles, and assorted books as they can practically carry. Specific instructions should be given in advance about how these materials are to be used. Since the team may need many more boxes of materials in the coming months than they can carry now, they should be instructed how to inform the center when and where to send more boxes. In the developed countries, that can best be done by phone or mail. In most other countries, cable is still the safest and fastest method.

Except for the literature and the amplifier, the team will travel very light. Traveling with too much luggage is extremely difficult and costly. Considering all the boxes of literature that must be taken, other luggage must be limited. Do not allow exemptions in this regard, as traveling light is an important part of the discipline.

Because the students will travel light, thought must be given ahead of time to clothes that are easy to care for (something that does not wrinkle easily and that dries quickly when washed).

Finances For the Field Training

The teams should be praying several weeks in advance of their departure for the Lord to supply the financial needs for their field training. They will expect to go in the manner of the Lord's original disciples (See Luke 9:1-6 & 10:7-11), that is with a limited amount of cash on hand and only the absolute essentials for daily life and ministry.

There is a very important reason for doing it this way. The Lord wants to do miracles for this team. They will *live of the Gospel* during the coming weeks and months — that is, the people to whom they minister will supply their physical needs (1 Corinthians 9:14). If those people don't respond, the Lord Himself will provide in other miraculous ways. This is an important part of the training, so don't rob the students of this experience.

The teams should not, generally speaking, sleep in hotels and eat in restaurants. Even if those amenities exist, that is not where the needy people to whom we want to minister are found. We must go where those people are and should expect to be housed and fed by the local people.

Assignments

Each team should be assigned an area of ministry,

sometimes a city, sometimes several villages. Once settled in that locale, the team will begin a systematic evangelization of the place. It will include ministry to:

Religious Leaders

We want to know the leaders and the churches that exist in the area so that we can refer those people who are reached by the team to a good church — if possible. Often these religious leaders themselves need spiritual help. With deep respect, the team members should probe the depth of the local leaders' experience, looking for ways to help them: with the Holy Ghost baptism, the gifts of the Spirit, knowledge of the coming of Christ, or perhaps, greater depths of personal holiness. In nothing else, they can be encouraged and blessed.

The team should share with these religious leaders books or booklets on the above-mentioned themes. If visiting the leaders opens the door to ministry in local churches, the team may accept, but that is not the primary goal and should take up a small part of the allotted time. The people we want to reach are usually not found in churches.

Political Leaders

The team should make a point early in the visit to witness and pray with, if possible, the mayors, governors, and any other political leaders of the region who can be reached. This may open many other doors. When it does, the team may enter.

The team should place a Bible in the hands of each

public official with the admonition that their people will be blessed if they learn and follow the Word of God. They should offer to give Bible studies in the City Hall or the Mayor's house during their stay in the city.

Further ministry to these officials will depend on the reception the team receives.

Educational Leaders

The team should witness to educational leaders, while arranging with them a time to speak in each classroom to the students. Usually, a public place like a school is not a good atmosphere to help someone receive the Holy Ghost baptism. So if there are teachers who show a genuine hunger for the deeper things of God, they may be prayed with privately or later in their homes or in the church. If a good supply of Bibles is on hand, one for each teacher who does not own a Bible is a worthy investment.

Students

In each classroom, the team members should give their testimonies, sing, offer a short message from God's Word, pray with the students and teachers, and give to each one a portion of the Gospel of John. A Bible and several good Christian books may be presented to the school library.

A schedule for such activities is usually arranged ahead of time with the educational authorities, and it is usually wise to abide by the agreed schedule. If not, you risk closing the door to future ministry.

Military Leaders

The team should visit military bases and get permission to have special sessions with new recruits and/or locally-based soldiers and officers. Each officer may be presented with a Bible, and each soldier with a Gospel. Bible Study courses by correspondence are usually well received in such an atmosphere because soldiers are lonely and have time to read and to correspond.

Acceptance of the Gospel message by military leaders often leads to many other ministries. The team leaders must be bold to propose possible activities.

Prisoners

Permission should be secured from prison authorities to witness from cell to cell and to preach to the inmates as a whole. This should be done weekly, if possible, during the time the team is in the city.

Gospels should be offered to most prisoners. Correspondence courses are also well received by prisoners. Bibles may be given in special cases, when there seems to be a genuinely positive response.

The Sick

The same type of ministry may be conducted in hospitals, with the precaution that hospitals all over the world are becoming more and more restrictive with such visits. Use wisdom not to offend the officials of the hospital, and stay within the limits of the permission you have been granted.

Others

The team should fill any spare hours with ministry in street meetings, witnessing in market places and from house to house. Tracts may be offered to everyone, Gospels to those who genuinely show interest in the message, and Bibles on a case-by-case basis — as there seems to be a genuine conversion.

More time should be spent with those who are genuinely saved, getting them filled with the Spirit and helping them to grow as much as possible in the Word of God.

A plan of evangelization must, of necessity, be different in rural areas of more primitive countries where, in some cases, mostly uneducated tribal people live. Emphasis in these areas should be given to winning chiefs, educated young people, and any other influential members of the tribe, to ministry from house to house and in public gatherings. Healing miracles are extremely important in these rural situations.

Much less time is necessary in small villages; but, since the villages are scattered, much time is spent in reaching them. This is therefore a physically taxing ministry, but a greatly rewarding one.

You are making progress in *Laying Biblical Foundations.*

- 28 -

LAYING BIBLICAL FOUNDATIONS
Materials for Evangelism

It sounds wonderful to be giving away Bibles and books and tracts and Gospels and to have portable amplifiers available for each ministry team. But how can the average church afford all that?

It is surprising how many agencies have been formed through the years by godly men and women to supply just this type of material for evangelism. There are many good Bible societies, tract societies, Christian printers and Christian publishers. There are even groups that specialize in providing portable amplifiers and tape players for evangelistic purposes.

These agencies have a certain amount of funds, either for free distribution of their materials or for subsidized pricing, and they are looking for dedicated men and women who will develop and execute a good systematic plan of evangelization. When they find such groups, they are usually eager to help in any way they can.

You never know what such a group might do for you. If they know that you are preparing workers, that you have a plan of action, and that you have limited funds for the project, they will usually either give you some materials or sell them to you at a very low price. It never hurts to ask. You lose nothing.

Having such materials can prove a blessing not only to a group of men and women training for the ministry, but for the entire membership of the church. If you have a supply of tracts, Gospels, books, and even Bibles, there are many good believers who will be happy to do the actual work of evangelization in your area. You might be surprised what excitement will be stirred up among your people.

If you are able to tap into a source of such materials, there are two important things to remember:

1. Don't be greedy. Share your materials with others. Use them to encourage your fellow ministers as well as your students. Having tools for the ministry is a great encouragement to any sincere believer. If you are generous and share the materials with others, God will give you more.

2. It is important to show your gratitude to those who gave to make the materials possible and to those who sacrificed to get them produced and made available to you. You can do this by send-

Materials for Evangelism

ing regular written reports of how the literature is being used and the response of the people to it.

Sending such a report should never be considered a burden. It is the least we can do to show our gratitude to those who have sacrificed to make it all possible. These people, whether we know who they are or not, are having a great part in our ministries, and they must not be forgotten.

It is for this reason that most of the agencies that supply printed materials to ministries all over the world require a written report. I find it sad that some of those who receive the materials are offended by this requirement, as if they are not trusted. This is not the point. How can we not express our gratitude?

The majority of supplying agencies suspend further shipments of materials if regular reports are not received, and I, for one, cannot blame them.

We are learning the secrets of *Laying Biblical Foundations.*

- 29 -

LAYING BIBLICAL FOUNDATIONS
The Graduation

Those who have completed the classroom training, the field training, and the correspondence study are worthy of graduation.

To create the proper atmosphere for the graduation service, have another several days of meetings with everyone present. This can be done during the final days of the week of prayer for new students, if you like. This should be a time of great rejoicing, and parents, family members, friends and pastors of the students should be invited. Special speakers may be secured for the occasion, if need be.

During the actual graduation service, each student may testify, if the group is not too large. A teacher

The Graduation

should remember them as they were a year earlier and recognize the change that God has made in their lives.

The diplomas (or certificates of achievement) may be very simple. They may not confer a degree, but only recognize that the student has successfully completed the course for ministerial preparation. Since the success or failure of the students' ministry reflects on the school, the church, and its leaders, a diploma should not be given lightly (to a student who has been continuously unruly in the field training, for example).

As the diplomas are given to the worthy students, have someone take some pictures, of individuals and of the entire group. Graduates will have many fond memories of their period of training and may want to purchase a copy.

Since the graduation is not really an ending, but a beginning of a new and exciting ministry for each of the graduates, be in prayer for several weeks or months before this event for God to give you wisdom to be able to help these young people find their place of ministry. Getting started is one of the most difficult aspects of the ministry for many. Therefore, an older, more experienced person or group of persons, should consider the matter in prayer and should be ready to assign the graduates a specific work or place of work, if they desire it.

Graduation is a big day, and is another important step in *Laying Biblical Foundations.*

- 30 -

LAYING BIBLICAL FOUNDATIONS
The Follow-Up

Follow-up is important in everything. There are many ways you can follow-up your Bible training to assure success.

First, by now you should have made yourself the friend and personal counselor of your graduates. Make sure they know that you are available anytime they need you — whether they are up or down, right or wrong.

Begin a regular correspondence with those who go to other areas. Send them a regular bulletin or magazine with testimonies, news of other companions in the ministry, encouraging messages, and announcements of upcoming activities.

Plan and announce regular conferences (every six months, or even every three months at first), a few days

The Follow-up 133

of fellowship with all the servants of God so you can know how they are doing. During such gatherings, those who are doing well can strengthen the weaker ones.

Visit your graduates occasionally, perhaps on special occasions. Preach for them. Encourage them. Bless them financially when you are able and led to do so (without making them financially dependent on you). Someone helped you get started too, and some day your students will return the favor.

Encourage all ministers to continue to grow through personal study, memorization of Scriptures and correspondence courses. Keep the names of all graduates on file. When one is not heard from for a while, write that person, visit them, pray with them. Help them to overcome any difficulty.

Continue this contact regularly. Don't lose contact with your spiritual children. Protect the investment you have made in *Laying Biblical Foundations.*

- 31 -

LAYING BIBLICAL FOUNDATIONS
Paid or Free?

The question of whether to charge for the training course seems to be a difficult one for many. The reason I hear most for charging is that: "People don't appreciate what they don't pay for." Personally, I don't agree with that viewpoint.

Somehow I can't picture Jesus charging His disciples for their training, and I can't picture the Apostles charging the various churches for the training they did.

Did Jesus charge to feed the multitude? Would they have appreciated it more if He had charged them? That thought seems absurd to me.

If you are developing a college of higher learning, then you must charge. But if you are imparting a ministry to the Lord's people, I would feel it more appropriate not to charge. Our Lord said, *Freely ye have received, freely give* (Matthew 10:8).

A free course has several advantages:

- From the beginning, the students are given to understand that the course is "by faith." If they pray and believe, there will be food for everyone. If not, they will all suffer. In this way, they learn faith as the course progresses.

- Because the student is not paying, it gives him a greater responsibility to work hard when he is assigned work and to respect the authority of those who are providing for him. It also makes it easier to dismiss erring, unruly, and misbehaving students.

- Since the local church itself will provide most of the needs of the students in preparation, it gives the members something else to work toward, a new challenge, and they are always blessed for their giving.

- Many of the students and their families will want to send food or money or both, as a sign of their gratitude, and they will be blessed more because they are not required to give it.

There is, however, a limit that you must not cross in this regard. I believe in providing a free room and free food for the students, but don't make the mistake of giving them soap, toothpaste, toilet paper, pens, and other such items. Those who have done this hindered the students in exercising faith for their own personal needs. Although they struggle at first, let them believe for these small personal necessities. It will build their faith. If you give them everything, they become too dependent on you.

The context of your course may require that you charge. For instance, if your program requires that each student have tapes and books, you cannot be expected to always provide them free of charge.

In Western countries, where funds are more readily available, the decision to charge and how much to charge may reach a very different conclusion. In the end, each training center and its leaders must decide whether or not to charge and how much to charge based upon the local circumstances and their own convictions.

The important thing is to get started *Laying Biblical Foundations.*

- 32 -

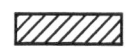

LAYING BIBLICAL FOUNDATIONS
A Word of Explanation on the Expulsion of Students

To some people, it seems very harsh to think of the expulsion or dismissal of a student from such a program. Expulsion! Dismissal! What terrible words!

I believe, however, that the concept of strictness in the training of full-time workers for the Lord's harvest is so important that I want to elaborate a little on it here, in closing this section. Not that I haven't already mentioned it enough.

On page 32 of Chapter 5, I said:

> *Those students who are unwilling to fast ... should be dismissed from the course.*

On page 33, I said:

> *Any student who is not 'pressing into' prayer should be counseled and prayed for. If the problem hindering a student cannot be resolved, he may eventually have to be dismissed. Nothing may be allowed to hinder the progress of other students ... .*

On page 34, I said:

> *When it is noticed that discipline has been breached, the teacher or director should immediately call the attention of the student to the problem. If the problem persists, expulsion must be considered as the best thing for the good of the whole group.*

On page 48 of Chapter 9, I said:

> *To the director falls the responsibility of disciplining unruly students. He must have both strictness and compassion to discipline the erring. If a student cannot be helped, it is the director's responsibility to dismiss that student before others are affected.*

The dismissal of a student is a serious matter and is not to be done lightly. The careful screening of students makes it much more unlikely that such a serious step will have to be taken. That is why I have emphasized (on page 52):

> *Not every student who applies for training can be*

A Word on the Expulsion of Students 139

> *accepted. There are many reasons for this. The two most important are:*
>
> *1. One bad student, one who is carnal or insincere, can adversely affect the entire group.*
>
> *2. As good stewards, we must be mindful to use wisely God's money and the investment of the time and talent of His servants, as well.*
>
> *The students for this course, therefore, should be carefully selected ... .*

And, in the section on *The Screening of Students*, on page 83:

> *The selection of the students for an intensive short-term Bible training program is as important, or possibly more so, than anything else about the course.*

As careful as you might be, however, experience tells us that occasionally it is necessary to dismiss a student who, for some reason, cannot find it in his or her heart to live by the rules of the course and who even attempts to wreak havoc on the whole group.

We must face the fact that Satan will do everything in his power to destroy the effectiveness of such a biblical training program. Wolves do creep in, attempting to spoil the flock. Even in Jesus' little group of twelve, one was found to be insincere. Jesus called him *"a devil"*:

Jesus answered them, Have not I chosen you twelve, and one of you is a devil? John 6:70

Although we know that Judas was ordained for an eternal purpose, he failed, and had to be removed from the group. We must make every effort to guard those who are sincerely preparing themselves for the ministry, and occasionally dismissing an erring student is part of that protection.

When it is noticed that a student is in serious spiritual danger, every effort must be made to help him recover. Those who are responsible must check the various areas of the student's spiritual life to see if the weakness can be found and corrected.

We must then give the student time to improve and strengthen his or her commitment, perhaps several weeks. Then, we re-evaluate the problem. If no significant progress is noted, we must consider resorting to dismissal — for the sake of the other students.

- To maintain the moral of the students

- To maintain discipline among the others

- To maintain the testimony and integrity of the institution

- To possibly save the soul of the person involved

I have actually had students who came and thanked me later for having been either rejected in the initial

A Word on the Expulsion of Students

screening or dismissed from class later. That hard action, they told me, shocked them into reality and made them get serious and seek God concerning their salvation and their ministry. As a result, some who were rejected or dismissed have become fine ministers today.

Although this is never an easy decision, it sometimes must be done and is part of successfully *Laying Biblical Foundations.*

Part II:

LAYING BIBLICAL FOUNDATIONS

Adapting This System to Other Circumstances

- 33 -

LAYING BIBLICAL FOUNDATIONS
The Differences

The formal Bible school setting is not the only place we have used this course. In most every country in which we have ministered, we have participated in church meetings, home meetings, jail meetings, office meetings and other types of meetings where this system of laying complete foundations proved to be very effective. It can be used almost anywhere, under the proper circumstances.

There are, of course, some differences when you apply this system of training outside of the classroom setting. Let us discuss some of those differences and how to deal with them.

Training Lay-People

The main difference is that when you are dealing with lay-people, you cannot make the same demands on their time, and you cannot expect them to abide by the same discipline. This necessitates drawing out the process over a much longer period of time. In some cases you will see the same results, while in others, you may not.

Some lay-people have so many job and family responsibilities that they cannot give the time necessary to study enough to make a practical change in their lives. But it is possible, and it is being done. Here are some ways you can do it:

What we accomplished in the classroom setting through rules and regulations can be accomplished through persuasion. Believe God to help you persuade people of their need for discipline and preparation. When they see others in outreach ministries and hear their testimonies of victory, they cannot fail to be moved to greater desire to be used in the same way.

When you find such people, impress on them how important it is to lay proper foundations and what happens to those who do not take the time necessary to do that correctly. Impress on them how important it is to develop good habits of being on time, of attending prayer and services, of working together for the good of the Kingdom.

New Christians seem to be much more open to these teachings. Those who have been around longer have sometimes gotten bored with the whole process and don't realize how much they need to be consistent and dedicated, but you can convince them.

The Methods Used

The same methods that we use in the full-time classroom and field training setting can be used, for the most part, in other settings.

Instead of requiring fasting and prayer, convince your students of the need to fast and pray. Set the example for them and expect them to follow. In churches where it is acceptable for a leader to call everyone to fasting and prayer, do it sometimes. Some people will never try to fast if it is not required or expected.

Personal discipline is just as important for the lay-person as it is for the full-time worker. It cannot be forced upon them, however, much as it is in the early part of the training of full-time workers. In the case of lay-people, it must be voluntary, so it must be forcefully taught and forcefully lived in front of them. Convince them that it is discipline which brings and keeps the anointing, without which there is no lasting work for God.

The memorization of Scripture, in the same way, usually cannot be required of lay-people, but its importance can be impressed upon them, and good examples can be set before them.

With lay-people, there may not be as much time for reading and reporting as is done in a classroom setting, but hungry people will not resent anything that is suggested for their spiritual growth.

Testing either cannot or should not be done in some settings. Each case must be judged on its own merits.

Teaching and preaching can and should be utilized in the training of lay-people. It is up to them, however, to faithfully attend these sessions. It is not uncommon for lay-people to miss services, some occasionally and others often, but there is no better teaching than to attend and flow with a lively, balanced Holy Ghost service. If a person will not attend services, he or she cannot be considered as a serious candidate for ministry.

Getting lay-people to come forward at every altar call at church meetings and to minister to others at the altar, in prayer and through the gifts of the Spirit, is important training in the ways of the Spirit.

Parenting is more difficult in an uncontrolled environment, but it is no less needed. We must make ourselves an important part of the lives of those we teach so that we can help them with their personal problems and can pray with them when they need our help.

The Atmosphere

The same atmosphere is needed for lay-people as for full-time workers. The problem is that if we are meeting in a home, in an office, in a restaurant, or in a jail, it is often impossible to control the atmosphere. You just have to do your best with what you have.

Some places have an atmosphere so bad that it is better to avoid them as training sites and to suggest a better place.

The Facilities

Many times you also have no control over the facility

where you conduct your training. In the places where people meet, there is often movement of people, coming and going, street noises, and other things that disturb. If the disturbance is too great, you might have to suggest that a better place be found. Sometimes you have no choice but to continue and to believe God to work for you — despite the circumstances.

The Minister/s

Regardless of where or with whom you conduct your Bible training, you need capable, holy, and Spirit-led ministers who have something to share. It is impossible to give what you don't have.

You may not need a director, and you may only need one teacher, but that person must have something meaningful to impart or you are performing an exercise in futility. Believe God to give you qualified teachers.

The Students

Although you may be teaching volunteers for the most part, it would be wise to still go through some screening process. You want to teach those who have a genuine desire for God and for service to God and who are mentally and morally ready to submit to further training.

A simple form of screening would be to ask applicants if they are willing to fast and pray regularly, to faithfully attend the teaching sessions, to submit to certain rules and to accept and perform assignments. If they agree, expect them to keep their agreement.

Many churches feel that they cannot turn anyone away. I understand their reticence, but I want to warn that accepting everyone who wants to study presents problems of inattention and lack of enthusiasm on the part of some. There are some people who attend everything, whether they have a burden to do something or learn something or not. Inviting everyone demands much more patience, discernment and tact on your part.

The Subject Matter

When teaching lay-people, I use the same subject matter, but I treat it on a different level. With lay-people we need to be more practical. We cannot go into as much detail, and we must compact our teachings even more, so that they will fit into the lesser time afforded us.

Textbooks and the Use of Prepared Teaching Materials

A Bible, of course, is a standard textbook for everyone. Other basic books can be suggested for outside reading and supplied at low cost — such as testimonies about Heaven, classics about prayer, and missionary classics. A library could contain one or two copies each of such books, plus Bible dictionaries, study Bibles, and maps (both national and world maps) — so that the students can develop a missionary burden and begin learning about both their own country and other countries.

Lay-people appreciate having something in their

hands. Study guides are very popular these days. Some material can be mimeographed or, in the more prosperous nations, prepared by computer and printed off.

Giving study materials to everyone, however, is not absolutely necessary. Each case must be judged on its own merits.

The Rules and Regulations for the Course

As we have said, this is one of the areas of greatest difference. Lay-people must be treated somewhat differently than full-time students for the ministry. The claims of the Spirit upon all are basically the same in working for God, whether in full- or part-time service: a dedication, purity of life and a desire for excellence.

The simple reality, however, is that very strict discipline imposed by instructors is not possible in these cases, as lay-persons are living in their own homes and are not subject to communal living values.

The Schedule

The schedule varies much from place to place. It depends totally on the availability of the teachers and the willingness of the students to attend the teaching sessions. In some places, students want to study several evenings a week. Some places use all day Saturday. Others have one night a week. We can only say that there is so much to be learned that we should do all that local circumstances will permit.

Preparation for the Classroom

The preparation for the classroom does not change, whatever the situation and whoever the people to which we are ministering. The methods of preparation we have outlined, in fact, are generally good for anyone in any ministry.

Testing

Testing can be done and should be done in certain circumstances. In other circumstances, however, it is not only unnecessary but would be counterproductive. After all, the proof of progress and success is in the individual's character development and the fruit of their ministry, not in what they have memorized.

Outside Activities

Pretty much the same outside activities can be planned for lay-people as for full-time workers. A formal class such as this can develop into a great outreach tool for the church into any needy area of the community. Consider ministry to jails, to drug addicts and other street people, to orphans, the elderly, the sick, and even ministry house to house. Give the students a taste of as many different ministries as possible. The experience will be invaluable for them, and somewhere along the line, they may discover their real calling in life.

Even before "training" is complete, arrange special meetings — street meetings, jail meetings, home meetings — so that trainees can see mature Christian workers in action and begin to participate with them. After all, you cannot "learn" to preach or to minister the gifts of the Spirit. You just do it.

Physical Work

It would not be wrong to use a class of lay-people in a work project; but, again, these are busy people, with many other responsibilities; so you are limited. Do at least one work project together for the church during the course to enable the students to feel the joy of serving the Lord with their hands. If it is possible, it might be wise to do something for the community, as well.

Sports

Since you are already severely limited in time with a group of lay-people, sports may be out of the question, and it may be unnecessary, since the average person has some physical activity in their day-to-day routine. If there is time and everyone wants it, it can't hurt anything to do something fun together once in a while.

The Field Training

Since it is very difficult to do the type of field training we have outlined with lay-people, similar activities can be planned in the local church or in other local churches. Get your people busy doing what they have learned. This ministry is to be shared, or it will be lost.

The Plan For Evangelization

This plan for evangelization can be done on a local level anywhere. It is, in fact, a very practical way for any local church to reach out to its community. If all we do is conduct services for those who are already saved and part of the Kingdom, are we really doing the Lord's work? He sent us to the world to share His love with all those who don't know Him. Sometimes we can do that in a church setting, but most sinners don't go to church. So, we must learn to go where the sinners are to be found and minister to them on their own territory, not insist that they must first come to us.

Using the plan for evangelization we have outlined here in conjunction with a formal program of training for lay-people may be the first step in getting your entire church involved in reaching out to the community around you.

The Graduation

It is probably just as important to hold a graduation service for lay-people as it is for full-time ministerial students, and it may be done in much the same way as we have suggested. However, because of the responsibilities lay-people have, you probably cannot spend several days, as we like to do otherwise.

The Follow Up

Again, the follow-up is just as important with lay-people as it is with full-time ministerial students. After you have invested much time and effort into their spiritual lives, you will want to protect that investment by maintaining contact with them and helping them in any way you can in the future.

Paid or Free?

The question of charging for a course of study or for materials for that course may be very different where lay-people are concerned. Most lay-people do have some financial means. The decision to charge or not to charge must be made by each local church. There are no hard and fast rules.

Materials for Evangelism

The special ministries we mentioned in the chapter, *Materials for Evangelism*, are very willing to help local churches with their outreaches to the community. Their policies usually follow a similar pattern: Materials are donated or subsidized for the developing countries. For the more affluent churches of the West, materials may be offered at cost or at a very reasonable price, usually depending on the amount of materials used.

When you make a request to one of these agencies, have a good plan. Then, stick by your agreement. Send in any promised reports and make any scheduled payments on time. In this way, you will fulfill your present commitment and will also keep the door open for the future.

The Expulsion of Students

As we have seen, when you are teaching lay-people, and the course is open to everyone, it is more difficult to apply strict discipline and to dismiss those who are not doing well. When we consider the seriousness of this matter, however, I don't think we should rule out the need, at times, to limit the participation to the genuinely sincere and dedicated. Let's get serious and move into action in God's harvest field.

Now, launch out. The harvest is ripe. Put the system you have learned to work for the furtherance of the Kingdom of God in your area of the world.

May God be with you, and may you reap a bountiful harvest, as you reap the results of your investment in *Laying Biblical Foundations*.

The Appendix

LAYING BIBLICAL FOUNDATIONS
Resource Materials For the Course

As I hope you have sensed in reading this book, I have a great love for the ministry of laying biblical foundations. I have participated in the training of workers on several continents, and I have also prepared materials for training workers. Everything I write I do so from the perspective of preparing laborers for the harvest fields. Some of the materials I have developed are available at the time of this printing, while others are in various stages of development.

Since this book contemplates the use of some of these materials, let me tell you about what is currently available and what will be available in the future.

Materials Now Available

Principles of Christian Faith, Volume I:
I have mentioned this book several times already and have given details about the material covered in it (See pages 71-73). The book is available in English and is being translated presently into Spanish and Russian.

Speaking In Other Tongues:
Since being baptized in the Holy Spirit and learning to walk and live in the Spirit, to pray in the Spirit and to exercise the gifts of the Spirit is such an important part of the life of an anointed disciple of Christ, this volume has proven an invaluable guide in this area of Christian training. It is simple, yet concise, and covers everything the Bible has to say about this all-important topic.

If we can help others to receive the things of the Spirit and to impart the things of the Spirit, we set off a chain reaction that will continue producing results long after we have personally left a particular location.

Who We Are In Christ:
This volume enlarges upon many of the teachings contained in the section **The Life of Christ** in the book *Principles of Christian Faith, Volume I.* It goes a step further by examining *Christ in us* and the largely-untapped resources that reside in us as a result of that mystery.

Secrets of Success:
This volume examines some of the overlooked aspects

The Appendix: Resource Materials For the Course 159

of the life of the Apostle Paul and how we can apply his secrets to our own lives and ministries. The book can be used in connection with teaching **The Acts of the Apostles** or as a separate study of the life of the first-century man of God.

Rescuing the 21st Century Marriage:
and
Rescuing the 21st Century Teenager:

In training sessions where we have neglected teachings on the family, students have complained about the omission. After all, students do marry and have children, and just because one is dedicated to the ministry does not make him/her immune to the difficulties facing families in these closing days of the twentieth century.

Although it is difficult to address every issue during a short course, it is wise to have some special sessions in which the problems of the modern family are addressed. These two volumes address many of the problems faced by those in ministry.

Leadership in the Christian Church:

At present, this is a three-ring binder containing the notes made available to the students for a thirteen-week course on the subject. The sessions were recorded on twenty-three one-hour audio cassettes. Both the tapes and the notebook are available. (In the future, this material will be included in the second volume of ***Principles of Christian Faith.***

Books in Various Stages of Preparation

Principles of Christian Faith, Volume II:
The first volume took some twenty years to prepare, but the second is well along. One of the subjects covered will be **Leadership in the Christian Church**.

What We Believe: Doctrine Made Easy:
This book enlarges upon the subject **The Principles** covered in note form in *Principles of Christian Faith, Volume I.*

Simple Faith:
This book enlarges upon the **Faith** subject covered in note form in *Principles of Christian Faith, Volume I.*

Prevailing Prayer:
This book enlarges upon the **Prayer** subject covered in note form in *Principles of Christian Faith, Volume I.*

Developing the Nature of Christ:
This book enlarges on the theme **The Teachings of Christ** covered in note form in *Principles of Christian Faith, Volume I.*

The Well-Balanced Christian Life:
A companion book to **What We Believe**, this book addresses the doctrinal excesses that often arise in immature believers.

Action and Reaction:
This book enlarges upon the subject **The Acts of the Apostles** covered in note form in *Principles of Christian Faith, Volume I.*

All May Prophesy: Taking the Fear Out of The Gifts of the Spirit:
A companion book to *Speaking in Tongues*, this volume delves more deeply into the biblical teachings on the gifts of the Spirit.

Forever or a Day:
This small volume is an orientation for new converts, an excellent piece to include in the materials for evangelism.

Other Resources

For the **Bible Survey** course, there are many excellent available resources. Many study Bibles now present an outline of each Bible book that contains precisely the materials I suggest.

There are many good books available concerning the **Signs of the Soon Coming of Christ**. One simple one is published and distributed by Christ For the Nations of Dallas, Texas.

There are several excellent and widely available books on the **History of the Church**.

If materials are not available to you on **Modern Israel**, consult your local Israeli Embassy. They will be happy to provide not only resource materials but films that you can show your students and maps and brochures that you can distribute.

Especially good for the study of **Mass Evangelism** is Morris Cerullo's *Handbook for the Harvest* and for **Evangelism** in general, T. L. Osborn's *Soul-Winning: Out Where the Sinners Are.*

Many materials are available for teaching **Other Religions and False Cults** and **Daniel and Revelation**.

Many good books of **Geography** are available. With the many changes in the world map, attention should be given to the date of publication.

Language Improvement can be taught from books used for local schools.

Consult with other Christian leaders in your area for materials you may be lacking. You can often borrow a good book long enough to glean from it the materials you need.

- **Notes** -

- Notes -

- Notes -

- Notes -